NICARAGUA

C A R I B B E A N

S E A

C O S T A

San
José
Escazú• ★

Limón

R I C A

PANAMA

Buenos
Aires

THE
LATIN AMERICA
MISSION
FIELD

D1384901

WHO SHALL ASCEND

THE LIFE OF R. KENNETH STRACHAN OF COSTA RICA

Other books by Elisabeth Elliot

NO GRAVEN IMAGE
THE SAVAGE MY KINSMAN
SHADOW OF THE ALMIGHTY
THROUGH GATES OF SPLENDOR

WHO
SHALL ASCEND

THE LIFE OF R. KENNETH STRACHAN
OF COSTA RICA

~~~~

BY ELISABETH ELLIOT

HARPER & ROW, PUBLISHERS

NEW YORK, EVANSTON,

AND LONDON

FIRST EDITION

LIBRARY OF CONGRESS CATALOG CARD NUMBER: 68-11732

A-S

To Elizabeth
who loved him

JUSTICE

I cannot skill of these Thy ways:
Lord, Thou didst make me, yet Thou woundest me;
Lord, Thou dost wound me, yet Thou dost relieve me,
Lord, Thou relievest, yet I die by Thee;
Lord, Thou dost kill me, yet Thou dost reprieve me.

But when I mark my life and praise,
  Thy justice me most fitly payes;
For I do praise Thee, yet I praise Thee not;
My prayers mean Thee, yet my prayers stray;
I would do well, yet sinne the hand hath got;
My soul doth love Thee, yet it loves delay;
  I cannot skill of these my ways.

GEORGE HERBERT (1593–1633)

AUTHOR'S NOTE

The sources for this biography include personal letters from the files of Harry and Susan Strachan and R. Kenneth Strachan, letters lent to me by his wife, Elizabeth, and children, Harry, Cathy, Robert, Clare, John, and Marie; an unpublished biography of his parents and the history of the Latin America Mission by R. Kenneth Strachan; the files of the Latin America Mission; personal interviews with many who knew Strachan, conducted by Harry and by the author; and Harry's diary of the days following his father's death.

I want to thank especially Elizabeth for her wholehearted cooperation and help; Harry, for a careful and thorough organization of all existing materials pertaining to his father's life; several who wrote me letters about Strachan's life; and Eleanor Vandevort for encouraging me in the writing itself and for proofreading the manuscript.

INTRODUCTION

Any book, including the novel and the biography, is the product of its author. Implicit within the book, to a greater or less degree, are the author's identity, his vision of reality, his understanding of life. For reasons that are not always very sound, more is often "read into" novels than into biographies, about the author's own philosophy. The novelist is charged with the whole guilt of creating his characters, causing them to act and be acted upon, giving them whatever virtues and failures they possess, and making the book "come out" as he wants it to. Oddly enough, however, biographers have sometimes assumed exactly the same responsibility, but have not been charged with the same guilt by their readers. This has been the case, for example, with certain Victorian biographies in which a particular view of the person written about was the generally accepted view, and the biographer merely chose material for inclusion in his book which would corroborate that view. By the judicious selection of favorable detail, then, he has caused his subject to act and be acted upon, he has given him virtues or failures, he has made the book come out, in accordance with the image previously established.

It is an awesome burden which the biographer takes up. Whatever he does will be a judgment—upon the subject most obviously, upon the biographer himself, and upon any who were associated with the subject. The Latin America Mission, of which Kenneth Strachan had been the director, asked me after he died to write the story of his life. In this sense only is this biography "official." When I explained to them that I could not consider it unless I were given complete freedom to write about him *as I saw him*, they did not withdraw their invitation.

And so I began—trying to *discover*, not to construct, the truth about this man. The careless—apparently, at times, haphazard—shape of the life unfolded itself before my eyes through his own writings and the testimony of those who knew him (I never saw him personally). Again and again I found myself tempted to ask what my readers would want this man to be, or what I wanted him to be, or what he himself thought he was—and I had to ignore all such questions in favor of the one relevant consideration: Is this true? Is this how it really was? And of course this is the question that any writer, of any kind of literature, has to be asking all the time.

We know in advance that we will not arrive at a complete answer. We are limited by deficiencies within ourselves. Our horizons are visible depending on where we are standing. The light is sometimes poor. Sometimes, when I was in the midst of a chapter or paragraph or sentence, a chink of light—perhaps very unexpected or even unwelcome *there*—would suddenly shine through, and I had to revise the whole section.

Possibly there is no better model for biography than the Bible. There it is perfectly plain that a true understanding of the world is not to be gained by pretending that things are other than what they are. If there is good, let it not be exaggerated. If there are evils, let us see what they are, and, if we will, let us bring to bear upon them the light of a Biblical faith, but let us not operate as though they simply did not exist and therefore needed no redemption.

I have tried to lay bare the facts of the case, answering the question, Is this what he was? with as much truthfulness, sympathy, and clarity, as I possess.

Franconia, N.H.
April, 1967

Note on the pronunciation of the name:
In an early letter to his fiancée Kenneth Strachan wrote, "The *ch* is pronounced by the Scots as if you had a hot potato in your mouth. The English pronounce it *Strawn*. The Americans mispronounce it *Strackan*." Most of Kenneth Strachan's family have by now settled for the American pronunciation, with a short *a*.

WHO SHALL ASCEND

THE LIFE OF R. KENNETH STRACHAN OF COSTA RICA

A student in Harley College in East London in the year 1900 approached a small blue-eyed girl named Susie who was studying in the same college and told her that God had revealed to him two things. First, that he was to go as a missionary to the Congo and second, that Susie was to go with him. The young man's name was Harry Strachan, tall son of a Scottish stonemason. The girl came from the Beamish family of Ireland, a long line of country people who had fought with Cromwell and been given in return a tract of land in Cork, which they own to this day. Half of the Beamishes got rich making beer and the other half got poor drinking it. Susan's immediate forebears belonged to the poorer half. They were good Anglicans, stanchly able to defend their tiny Protestant community in the heart of Catholic Ireland. Susan had somehow begun to attend a little Methodist chapel where the hymn-singing, praying, and Bible reading were of a different temperature from what she was used to. She was warmed and inspired there, and found herself at last preparing for missionary service in the same college with Harry Strachan. His abrupt announcement of God's revelation to him and her responsibility regarding it must have astonished her, but not for a moment did it confuse her. Nonsense! was the gist of her reply. God had already issued His instructions. She was going to Argentina, she informed Harry—and to Argentina she went. With admirable singleness of mind Harry pursued his efforts to join a mission in the Congo but was finally rejected on medical grounds, and within nine months he landed in Argentina. A year later he and Susie were married and began their missionary work in Tandil, a frontier town

1

of twelve thousand people—mostly European—on the pampas where there was a struggling Protestant congregation of fourteen people. They tackled the job with heart and soul, but heart and soul of the two Strachans were too big to fit tidily into the pigeonhole of this local work, and Harry soon began to cover the surrounding plains with preaching and the distribution of Gospel literature.

They waited seven years for children, and then three were born in rather rapid succession. Robert Kenneth was the first, born in 1910, and although his mother had prayed for a girl, she had thought she heard God say, "Suppose it's a boy?" and she had agreed that that would be all right. She felt quite sure that God would let her have what she wanted the second time, but again had to settle for a son. The third child, however, was a daughter, whom they named Grace, and Susan was content.

Of his brief years in Argentina Kenneth remembered the great grasslands with the howl of coyotes and wolves at night; his father singing loudly as he drove a buggy over hills and flats, through sloughs of mud and stagnant water on his way to preach at some distant ranch; small meetings with ranchhands and large tent campaigns with village people. Often he went away for long trips and Kenneth, at the age of six, put down on paper something of the desolation he felt during those endless absences:

> dear papa, it is very cold, come home soon
> Kenneth X X X X
> Harry X X X X
> Grace X X X X
> dear papa come
> dear papa come
> Kenneth
> dear papa come home
> Kenneth.

Pastoral work, even with the opportunities to visit distant areas, was not enough for Harry Strachan, and by the time Kenneth was seven the family had gone to the United States for a furlough, where the parents decided that they must resign from the Evangelical Union of South America and begin itinerant evangelism. They visited Central America and found that San José, Costa Rica, which seemed to them a good center for headquarters, had only two missionaries, both women, and these two were about to leave.

"We were terribly burdened with the tragedy of it," wrote Harry, and he and Susan decided that this was the place to settle.

"Settle" is hardly the word, however, for what the Strachans did. A little wood-burning locomotive pulled the family up the mountains from the Atlantic coast in the midst of the rainy season of 1921. Harry installed them in a rented house on an unpaved street where the gutters overflowed and children sailed paper galleons under their windows. Within four days he had left them again for Guatemala, providing his wife with a hundred dollars in cash and a check which he had forgotten to sign. He was a very busy man—a powerful, driving man with a one-track mind, and he had important things to do. The evangelization of Latin America could not wait. Susan would make out. Of that he had no fear.

Early mornings with the creaking of ox-carts in the street and the blowing of the animals pushing against their wooden yokes; the milk boy on his horse, surrounded by women with saucepans; the smell of wood smoke from the kitchen next door; afternoons with the sound of a piano mournfully playing Chopin's funeral march; the lashing of the tropical rains on the roof and on the *higuerón* trees that swished and bent in the wind. Evenings, and again the creak of carts and sucking of oxen hoofs in the mud of the roadway, dim lights showing through narrow windows of low houses, the damp cold of night three thousand feet above sea level. This was where Kenneth Strachan lived, the city he would call home for the rest of his life. The school he went to was Methodist and nearly all of his friends were Latin. One of them recalls him as very small for his age, very handsome, but otherwise very like any other boy. He did things like jumping from a roof with an open umbrella, tying a purse on a string in order to yank it out of the grasp of the first person who tried to pick it up. He and his brother Harry played in giant drainage tubes and had to be thrown out of them by the police. They rang doorbells and ran away, called out insulting remarks to passersby while hiding themselves from view, played basketball and baseball, read books alone in their rooms, collected stamps, and went obediently to Sunday School. Ken had a little garden which he planted and earnestly prayed over.

Their mother was totally absorbed with the founding of a girls' school while her husband was away, and wrote to a friend,

"I cannot doubt that this thing is of God, and so I know that He will send us enough money to keep the girls when He sends them to us. Though I am ashamed to ask Him, yet it would be just like the Lord to assure the support of these girls before school begins so that I could arrange with them about getting here. What I mean is that I am ashamed to ask Him in the way of a test, or as further proof that this is His plan. The fact is, that I have asked Him to do it on the ground that He must carry on what He has begun because I cannot do it."

Whether her faith exceeded her determination or vice versa would be difficult to say, but Susan Strachan got what she wanted, and the school opened. When her own children needed help with their homework they learned to ask Mary France, the single lady missionary who lived with them. They were taught the importance of their parents' work, which had been named the Latin America Evangelization Campaign (LAEC), and when their father left them for his third evangelistic journey, Ken handed him a letter to read on the train. "Dear Papa," it read, "We are happy to have a father who serves the real God. So we want to help you on your journey by all the money we can give you." Years later the frayed letter still contained a one-colon bill (worth about twenty-five cents then) which had been enclosed.

Kenneth remembered the days when Father came home. Mother would sparkle and the children would catch her enthusiasm. He got off the train, tall and smiling and tired, with his leather valise looking a little more worn, his suit a bit more wrinkled, his moustache in need of a trim. But he was very happy and proud to see his family, and seldom took the trouble to describe in detail what must have been exhausting travels. But not long after his return he would shut himself in his study to work for long hours, appearing at mealtimes and for the ritual of afternoon tea. He had no time for small talk. There would be serious discussions over the tea table between him and Susan, sometimes leading to spirited argument. Finally Harry's heavy eyebrows would converge and he would say, "My dear, I've said the last word," and that would be that. "Dearie" was the most affectionate term he used for his wife, and that not often. She sometimes referred to him as "Hub" but both avoided public display of affection to each other or even to the children. In fact, God and love, two subjects profoundly revered in the family, were rarely mentioned at all in a personal rather than theoretical context.

Harry's faith in his wife's executive ability and business sense was great if not actually superstitious, and he gladly left all matters pertaining to the establishment and management of the home mission base in her hands. He himself was swamped with correspondence relating to his travels and campaigns, and he spent most of his time at a desk, in what looked like a hopeless muddle of papers and books. Trifles like haircuts he never thought of, but when reminded would intemperately have the whole business done with by having his head nearly shaved. His wife did his packing for him when he went off on trips, and had to see not only that he had plenty of handkerchiefs but also cologne to sprinkle on them. The buying of cologne, in their circumstances, must have taken some careful advance planning.

One of Susan's projects was the purchase of a farm which she hoped might ultimately contribute to the income of the mission as well as provide food. The property was ten miles outside of the city, on a hillside overlooking a vast sweep of mountain and fruitful valley, the Meseta Central. Whenever Kenneth got the chance, he went to the farm with his mother or with those she had delegated to do her errands. He explored every inch, "jumping from stone to stone in the streams, rhyming, singing poetry to myself, dreaming," he wrote in later years. "I have a romantic and impractical streak about a mile wide. I used to love to play imaginary games of adventure by myself. I fought through the Crusades with wooden swords. I settled in New England with the Pilgrim Fathers and drove Indians off, I skulked through the woods with the Deerslayer and some of the rest of Fenimore Cooper's heroes, and best of all I used to love sailing the seas in search of pirate treasure. I remember that at night until I was called in to bed I would lie under a bush in the back yard with a wooden gun in my arms, guarding a lonely outpost and popping off any Indians that might come into range."

CHAPTER 2

When Kenneth was fifteen years old his parents had him baptized and his father took him to the States. During the last hour of the journey, the train ride from Chicago to Wheaton, Illinois, it occurred to Mr. Strachan that there were certain facts which a boy of fifteen, leaving home for the first time, really ought to be acquainted with. It was a painful hour, but he got through it, and shortly after their arrival he had enrolled his son in Wheaton Academy and said goodbye.

The boy wore short pants (his mother had outfitted him, as she thought, quite suitably), and weighed less than a hundred pounds. Each morning he would stretch himself in front of his mirror and wonder if he had yet reached five feet. But he was on his own, for the first time in his life, and although the apron strings were still very strong he felt glad that they were at least a little lengthened. His mother wrote faithfully to him every week, in spite of being always "terribly" or "desperately" busy with the work of the school (which had now become a Bible Institute), the publication of a magazine called the *Evangelist*, and the supervision of the farm. When she had opportunity she checked up on him through friends. She wrote to Ken that she was asking a certain lady to go and see him "or perhaps you could go and spend the day with her in Chicago." No, begged Kenneth, "please don't ask her to see me before she goes back because she pokes around and asks me if my shoes are always clean, etc. She is very nice but we don't fit well."

For a schoolboy Kenneth did remarkably well in corresponding with his mother, accounting for every penny spent and reporting dutifully on his activities from week to week. There were a few occasions when his letter did not arrive, and on one of these his mother wrote, "As you have missed another mail I suppose that your conscience was troubling you. Now, son, quit that business of missing mails. I just cannot stand it when the mail comes in and your letter is not amongst the others. I hope you will realize this and not miss anymore."

Sometimes the boy missed a mail because he did not know what to write about. He hardly dared to say much of the two things which alone held any interest for him—stamp collecting and baseball. His parents were suspicious of the American emphasis on sports and had had to admonish both their sons continually not to spend so much energy on games that they had none left for the "serious business of study." This was the beginning of one of the more severe conflicts which lasted throughout Ken's life—that of being expected to fill a certain bill which in his heart he was convinced he could not fill. He was conscientious and earnestly desired to please and set at rest those he loved, but he could not abide hypocrisy. How could he appear to be interested in what did not in fact interest him at all? Repeatedly he wrote to apologize for disappointing his parents, and they wrote repeatedly to remind him of their hopes.

"I don't think, Kenneth, that you are doing as well as you should with only four subjects," wrote his mother, whose understanding of the American system of education was very vague and led her to believe that Kenneth was shirking his duty by not taking ten subjects as Harry was doing under the Costa Rican system. "Your grade oscillates between eighty and eighty-seven. Is it because you are not working hard enough? I would expect you to get always above ninety and hope you may be able to top your class. Last night when I was talking to Harry about his marks he said, 'There are others lower down than me.' What a standard to have! It should always be the upward look, and no rest while there are others above you. Your place in life, son, if you will take it, is at the top of the class—whatever the class may be. I remember a poem that ran, 'There's always room at the top, my boy, there's always room at the top.' Of course there is because most people will stay comfortably somewhere along the route and do not exert themselves to get to the top. But your place is up there, Kenneth. Don't let basketball or any other ball keep you back from it." And again, "Time is going, Kenneth, and you are now seventeen and must settle down seriously to work. We are glad for you to play tennis and all the rest but this must be the smallest part of your program. Harry and Grace are coming on and we shall not be able to give them their chance if you spend too much time on the road." His mother was not satisfied with his handwriting and told him that he must learn to make straight lines and to write more legibly. Harry was not doing what she expected in schoolwork either, and she wrote to Kenneth to urge his brother to work harder. "Put it strongly. Of course you will not tell him I asked you to do it."

Money was Kenneth's biggest preoccupation, and month after month he sent his mother the bills for board, room, laundry, and fees. These sums seldom varied, yet she never sent payment in advance and frequently reminded her son to be sure to let her know how much he would need. As for incidentals, she seemed unaware that there were such things for a growing boy in school away from home. He did persuade her, by the time he was in his junior year, that long pants were a must, but when he asked for an overcoat ("because, Mama, it really does get colder up here than you realize") she sent him a check for twenty-five dollars out of which he was to buy the coat and any other clothing he might possibly need for the whole year. At Christmastime she wrote, "I am aghast that it is time to send you another check. I am enclosing five dollars for laundry, five dollars for Christmas from Papa, and five dollars from me for Christmas. Be sure to buy things you really *need.*" When she received his Christmas gift, she wrote, "Why did you spend so much money on us, son?"

Frequently Mrs. Strachan described the large building projects she was engaged in, and the huge sums of money necessary to finance them. Although Kenneth probably knew that mission funds and personal funds were kept separate, it must at times have been difficult for him to understand why the God who could supply thousands of dollars for a new clinic or church could not seem to furnish a schoolboy with money for socks. He did not complain, and there is no hint in his letters that he felt his parents were being parsimonious. They themselves received a total monthly stipend of fifty dollars. Ken did his best to supplement the allowance they gave him, and got a job at twenty cents an hour in a restaurant. At this point he opened two bank accounts, in which, when he reported them to his mother, he had thirteen dollars for tuition and fees, and ten dollars for clothes, each account drawing 3 per cent interest. He took five hours' wages to buy stationery so that he would not have to write to his mother on scratch paper. Once a job was offered to him which would involve Sunday work. He was tempted by the higher pay, but was unsure of the moral implications of working on the Lord's Day. His mother's advice to him was, "Drug stores are more soda and candy businesses than anything else and I would not think a Christian ought to serve in that sort of thing. If the Sunday work was only and strictly the delivery of medicines, I think perhaps there would be no objection. But I would like you to pray about this yourself. . . . The important thing is for you to be true to Christ whatever else happens."

He replied, "It was a good opportunity but I failed to get to the interview because I was doubled up with a bilious attack. Maybe it was God's will. I knew that the seventh day is for rest."

To add to his difficulties with grades and money, he suspected that the college treasurer was cheating him, and his housemother interfered with his affairs. "I don't like the idea of that old woman trying to tell me what to do. It's none of her business." His health was never perfect. A succession of headaches, nosebleeds, stomach upsets, unexplained pains, boils, pimples, styes, and frequent colds made life a burden to him and reminded him of his discontent and loneliness. "On Mondays I wait for the postman, and on other days I wait for Mondays. . . . I have been writing Papa weekly but so far have received only one letter."

Many of his letters reflect a wistful longing to get back to Costa Rica. He always wanted to know about the farm and the animals, his dog, his brother and sister and Latin friends, and he hoped that his life work might be there. "I don't know if it's God's will but I always have a feeling that Costa Rica is the place for me. Maybe that is just because my home is there." He referred several times, during high school days, to "when I become a missionary," and his mother answered, "That would be a great joy to us, son, if it be God's plan for you. That would mean that you would be a missionary like your father. (The last part of that sentence is the best, son, for there are few missionaries like your father.)"

Kenneth's three years in Wheaton Academy passed without his ever writing of one unqualifiedly "good" time. Even the best of times, sports events or dinners in the homes of friends, were described as "pretty good." A chapel speaker of national repute was pretty

"a ∧ good minister." He had a "fairly" good time on Saturday night, and hoped that a certain social occasion would be "not too boring." He lived for the day when his brother Harry would come to the States and go to school with him. "I hope I can find a room in a private home for Harry and me where we can work. And then, in a private home, you get to be part of the family, too." Each school year ended with his being "tired and disgusted with everything." During the summers he found work in Christian conference centers or camps, and from one of these he wrote:

"I'm tired of this rotten cooking which makes me sick. The milk is the kind they feed to hogs. I've had boils and styes and stomach trouble and the toilets are a mile away. I sure don't like this place. It might be a good place spiritually and morally for the guests but it sure isn't if you're thrown in with the help. One thing I notice is that the bosses talk about being Christian but their actions are not Christianlike. It makes me sick. The other Sunday they had a disagreement whether to open the candy booth or not—B. against it and S. for it. Finally they compromised on selling the ice cream at the lunch counter. Their reason was that people would go downtown anyway. You see, they are losing money here. Pretty soon they started dropping in soft drinks to sell, also, S. and B. both coming around to see we were getting much more money. . . . What makes me mad is the hypocrisy around here. Next year can I stay at Wheaton and work?" At the end of this summer of hard work and low pay Kenneth wrote an account of what he had earned, adding that most of it had been stolen by one of the workers so that he was left with thirteen dollars. He wondered if his mother might be able to send him money for a pair of pants, since he had just one pair for school.

His mother, far away geographically, pressed with immediate cares in her own work, unfamiliar with America and its way of life, little realized what her son's actual needs were, though she did her best to fulfill her duty as she saw it. His father was a faint shadow most of the time, traveling in areas from which communication was often impossible. His mother would write that she did not know where Father was, that she had not heard from him for two months, or that she had no idea when to expect him home. Ken sometimes learned of his father's whereabouts only through the news in *The Evangelist*. When she spoke of mission projects it was with the first-person singular pronoun. "I am having a new clinic built," or "I am getting on well with the building of the Templo." But the usual tone of the letter was by no means self-centered. There were frequent expressions of her love and concern.

"I am sure that you know how much I love you, son of mine, and that I am always praying for you. I would have enjoyed my holiday much more if you could have been with us but some day I hope we shall all have our holiday together once more. Are you praying as I suggested that the Lord may show you what calling in life He wants you to follow? He will do it in a very clear way if you make it a matter of continual prayer. The most important thing in life is to be in the place and doing the work that He has chosen for us, for otherwise there will be no satisfaction and very little success in what we do. My prayer for you, Kenneth, is that your desire more and more may be to know Him and serve Him. There is nothing else worth having in life. I would rather see you the humblest worker for God than the President of the United States out of God's will and service. What will the world and all its glory be worth when Jesus comes for His own? It is then that the real things will be made manifest and then it will be shown that the world and all its pleasure and glory are but poor tawdry baubles that men have chased to their own destruction. So, Kenneth, keep step with Christ day by day and you will have no heartaches either now or hereafter.

Lots of love, son, and many kisses, from
Mother."

CHAPTER 3

Ken returned toWheaton in the fall of 1928 after a summer in his beloved Costa Rica. Things looked considerably brighter for him for a while, first because his brother Harry had accompanied him back to the United States and was enrolled in Wheaton Academy, and then because Ken was now a freshman in college. He began to attend the weekly college prayer meetings and responded enthusiastically to "altar calls." He even managed to get to early morning prayer sessions for a time, but then a job from six P.M. to one A.M., for which he earned one dollar a night, necessitated his sleeping a little later. He felt a brotherly responsibility for Harry, and reported to his mother, "Harry has been doing pretty good about prayer meeting. But I'm going to make him quit basketball as he is not in condition to play." He advised her against scolding Harry about his failure to write as regularly as Ken. "A bawling out is not a very good incentive to letter writing. In my case it never was."

As the freshman year wore on Ken's letters home gave evidence of the same discontent and boredom he had felt in the Academy. He was still plagued by his small stature and wrote anxiously to inquire whether his sister Gracie was growing taller. Again he wrote of health troubles, in one letter complaining of cold sores, bad wisdom teeth, a sore throat—"I'll soon be dead." He had to be fitted for glasses and was told to wear them all the time. This was another trial, because "they make me look simpy, silly, and sappy."

He had gone through high school without losing much time because of girls ("I have yet to meet a woman who comes anywhere

12

near being your equal," he had written to his mother), but in his
freshman year of college he succumbed to custom and confessed, "I
did go around a few times and I'm sorry to say we weren't entirely
conventional, but I got sick of that stuff right away and haven't been
out since." His sister wrote to him now and then from Costa Rica,
confiding to him her restlessness and wish that she were out from
under the parental thumb as he was. He wrote back affectionately
most of the time, revealing a genuine admiration for his kid sister
and expressing his hope that she, too, would come to Wheaton, but
once when she wrote an especially frank letter he rebuked her for
"sentimental trash" and "wayward sinner sob stuff."

During the summer between his freshman and sophomore years
Ken worked at Minne Wonka, a girls' camp in Wisconsin, hauling
wood and ice and cutting lawns. "I like this place fairly well, the
people are nice, food good, scenery fine, climate agreeable, everything else passable," he wrote. Everything, that is, except the woman
who supervised the dining room. "She is continuously letting her
tongue run away with her, her voice is unpleasant, her head empty."

Grace arrived during the summer and the three Strachans spent a
week at the Bible conference that Ken had written so disparagingly
of the year before. This time, because he was a guest and not
"thrown in among the help," and undoubtedly because Harry and
Grace were with him, he actually had a "keen" time. But the prospect of returning to college and studies was a bleak one, and he
suggested to his parents that he take a year off. His father thought
the idea acceptable, but assured Ken that "Mama wouldn't hear of
it." Ken gave her his reasons: (1) so that he might see school from
a different viewpoint, and (2) so that he would know better what he
wanted to do. Papa was right. Mama wouldn't hear of it, and back
to Wheaton Ken went, feeling that the summer had profited him in
some areas. "Have no fear. Your little son has learned a lot this
summer and not only has his table manners down to a T but also is
well at ease when at the table. I really believe I am getting over the
'shrinking violet' stuff also." He began eating in the dormitory that
year, which meant that he encountered women three times a day.

His enthusiasm reached a new peak at Thanksgiving when he
allowed himself to report that they had had a "lot of fun and horse

play and one good square meal." Christmastime, however, found him refusing several invitations for dinner and going instead with a friend to an Italian restaurant in Chicago where the meal "cost plenty but was nice." He was glad when Christmas was over, for he had had too many of them away from home and was tired of it. He hardly seemed to have expected the family in Costa Rica to have had a better time. "I suppose you received a lot of gifts. I hope some of them will be of use to you." But his pessimism alternated with hopefulness, and he looked forward to his parent's coming to Wheaton in the following year, suggesting, in case they had not thought of it, that it might be nice if they would plan for Harry and him to live with them when they came. The plan did not work out, but to a certain degree Ken and Harry's need of a home was met when they were able to visit the Dennisons of Johnstown, New York. Alfred Dennison was a lawyer who had four children. His wife had invited Mr. and Mrs. Strachan to their home years before, when the Strachans had left Argentina, and it was while staying there that Harry and Susan Strachan had first envisioned the Latin America Evangelization Campaign. Mrs. Dennison's mother-heart went out to the lonely Strachan children and she often had them stay with her in the spacious old Victorian home in Johnstown, or at their summer cottage on a nearby lake. Sometimes the entire Strachan family were her guests, and she remembers the parents, sitting at a table surrounded by their papers, unaware that it was mealtime and their hosts were waiting for them. Mrs. Dennison was "Aunt Marguerite" to Ken and Harry and Grace, and her home was the scene of some of their happiest days in the States. Years afterward, when Ken visited Johnstown, he walked around reliving those days: "the place in front of the courthouse where I ran out into the street and a car ran over my ankle (never did tell Mother), the ten-cent store where Harry, Grace, and I bought each other Christmas presents; the place where I saw my first Hallowe'en pumpkin, with a lantern in it; the town chimes . . . East Caroga Lake, where the old boathouse was, where I lay for hours fishing for rock bass; I saw the marsh where we picked cranberries and caught an occasional grasshopper for bait."

Strachan's junior year in college saw a significant spiritual crisis.

"I had meant to keep still about this bit of news but feel too glad about it to shut up," he wrote to his mother. "Last night (November 30—you can mark the date) R. K. Strachan gave up a losing fight and surrendered to Christ." At Swedish Church he had stayed after the service and knelt with a group of friends, first with the intention of sneering at their earnestness, and then capitulating to the urgent plea to surrender. "The Bible seems new to me, and God is with me to help me. I think I've never really been converted before."

This experience was followed by a serious effort to put conviction into practice, and Ken began attending prayer meetings again, giving occasional testimonies before the students (though not often, he said, because he hated hypocrisy and feared backsliding); he participated in street meetings, Gospel teams and Bible studies; he even wrote a letter to a convict telling him how to repent. For the first time, he told his mother that he had a "wonderful time"—not at a football game, not at a school party, but at a hymn sing and prayer meeting, held in a car on the way to mission work in Chicago. This led to the decision of his life's work. In March of 1931 he wrote, "Without much thought or prayer, I suddenly realized that my work would be in missionary service, and I have a feeling it will be in Costa Rica." Early practice in missionary work included bringing several fellow students to a profession of faith in Christ. His roommate, however, proved intractable, and Ken decided that he must separate himself from him. "To stay with R. as my roommate would be to compromise my stand. I have stayed long enough to be a testimony but since he still goes his way, I'm looking for another roommate."

Harry was in the hospital with a high fever when Ken decided to write something that he had tried in vain to tell Harry face to face. "Don't get scared. I am not going to start preaching at you but it's easier for me to say what I mean in writing rather than orally. To be frank, and you'll admit it, the way you are going on now you won't get anywhere. (This isn't scolding, we're just talking it over calmly.) Don't think I'm trying to talk to you from a higher level or anything —because I went through the same thing myself, and it took the Lord Jesus Christ to snap me out of it. However, we won't discuss that part of the question. The thing is this, Harry. You're getting old

enough now so that you should be fairly dependable and steady—
also so that you should know when to go tearing and when not. I've
had several teachers come up to me and ask why you hadn't been
coming to class anymore. Cutting class is a bad habit, Harry, and I
have it too, but if possible you ought to break it. And Harry, I know
that you've got enough guts and self-will to go to class if you make
up your mind. Now's the time to settle down and do some good
work in classes, for when spring comes you'll have a harder time yet.
Well, we won't say anything more about it, except that I know you
can do it and really dig into your studies if you make up your
mind."

Later exhortations from the older brother included the suggestion
that Harry not miss any opportunity to do something for Mama, and
that he make out a schedule of study time in order to get his homework done. When their father paid them a visit during that winter he
was pleased to hear of Ken's spiritual progress, and concerned to
know that Harry had made no such commitment. A heart-to-heart
talk with him satisfied the father, but Ken wrote to his mother
shortly afterward, "Father got Harry under the stress of the moment,
and it wasn't real." Ken talked with Harry and felt that he then
made a "real" decision, but was not so sure of its reality when he
found that his brother still liked "that old jazz music." "In case you
think of it," he wrote, "pray for three kids up here: Gracie, Harry,
and Kenneth." Grace, who was by this time a student at Wheaton
Academy, had also tried to tune in to her older brother's wave
length, but he saw that she felt rushed into it and was miserable.

Mrs. Strachan was quick to take advantage of her son's eagerness
to serve the Lord by suggesting that he go to seminary to prepare
himself. This started an argument by correspondence, for Ken was
living for the day when he would be free of schoolwork, and another
three or four years of study held no appeal for him whatever.
Shrewdly, he based his argument on Scripture. "Look up Colossians
2:8," he wrote. ("Beware lest any man spoil you through philosophy and vain deceit, after the tradition of men, after the rudiments
of the world, and not after Christ.") "It's awfully easy for a seminary to fall into that. And in Luke 10:30-37 it shows that the priest-
hood has lost its favor with God. He is turning to laymen. I know
there are plenty of weak spots in my argument. . . ."

Toward the close of that school year the old depression began to descend again and Ken wrote that he had tried to spend an hour every morning reading the Bible but could not get much profit from it. He had been sports editor of the college yearbook, and when other staff members were elated to see their finished work off the press, he "didn't even want to look at it." He found no satisfaction in the job he had done. He quit accompanying Gospel teams, but made it clear that he was not going back on his stand. "I have a vivid recollection of my experience with Christ, and I'm glad I'm saved. Pray."

Harry, who for a brief time had seemed to respond to his brother's influence, cooled off again, and though Ken "tried to have a talk, as you suggested, he doesn't seem to care. . . . If he came up to camp with me I could keep an eye on him." But instead of going to camp, Harry went to Costa Rica that summer. He was taken ill during the spring and had to leave school and go home. Ken thought that he would be responsible for making the preparations for Harry's journey south, and inquired of his mother what they should be. To his surprise and chagrin, he found that Harry himself had handled quite capably all necessary arrangements, including getting a visa. What a "lucky stiff" or "lucky cuss" his brother was! Ken found it harder than ever to stick to his books after this, and shortly after learning that Harry had had appendicitis at home, Ken suffered from an acute pain in his right side which worried him so much that he went to the doctor. No, said the doctor, it was not appendicitis, but he had better cut out heavy lifting.

He got the same job he had had the previous summer at Minne Wonka, and wrote of a "great time" swimming and diving. But life was not made up only of swimming and diving, and Ken thought that he saw a great cleavage between certain areas of his life. Spiritually, he felt that he had backslidden "after that splendid time with the Lord last winter." The term "backslide," as Ken had been taught, referred to any cooling of one's spiritual temperature, resulting from any failure to do what seemed to be God's will (for example, failure to attend college prayer meetings or have one's daily "devotions") or from any deliberate infringement of His laws. Wheaton College required its students to sign a pledge that they would not drink, smoke, play cards, dance, attend any kind of theater, or join a secret society. To break any part of this pledge would be regarded, by Ken and by most Wheatonites, as disobedience not only to the college but also to God. Ken's references to his own "backsliding" are seldom specific, so it is usually a matter of pure conjecture whether he meant sins of omission or commission.

"My highest ambition," he told his mother, "is to be as completely yielded to the Lord as you and Papa are." The discrepancy between his condition and his ambition could hardly help creating new tensions and it is not surprising that skin eruptions and stomach cramps returned, and his letters were gloomy once more. "I can hardly pray. I'm hard as a rock. I don't feel like writing. I want to go home."

Home was like a beacon light to him. Always it shone dimly as the goal of the future. When school was out, or when summer vacation came, or when he graduated, *sometime*, he would get back to his longed-for San José. Then, when he believed that God Himself was actually calling him to return there as a missionary, the light shone brighter. Letters from his mother cheered him and he felt protective and concerned at the least hint that all was not well with her. She was thrown from her horse once, and he scolded her and told her to be careful. She was too busy, he feared, and wrote, "Don't work so hard, Mama. You'll break down. Button up your overcoat, you belong to me!"

He noticed that she always signed herself "Mother," and he tried calling her that in one or two letters, thinking perhaps she preferred it, and it was, after all, more fitting for a boy who was twenty-one years old now, but soon he reverted to "Mama" again. "Papa is so formal in his correspondence it makes you want to laugh, though you usually end up with a catch in your throat," he wrote to her.

The summer came to an end; Ken was displeased with his boss at camp for "tightness on money—even though I did extra work." He returned to college with no heart left for study. On September 29 he wrote:

"Dear Mama,

"I know you will have been worrying and been disappointed at not receiving any mail from me for so long, but I just couldn't seem to write, because I wanted to go home rather than go to school. If it had not been for that $250 deposit I would have been home by now.

Harry, Kenneth, and Grace Strachan, about 1922

The Strachan family, about 1930

Kenneth, Grace, and Harry in Tandil, Argentina

The only reason that stopped me was because I didn't want to have to write you a long letter of explanation asking you to fix it up with the Costarican government. I was going to do all my explaining when I got home. I suppose you'll think it was just a fancy of mine—if you do, you'll never know how close you came to having me on your hands this year.

"So instead I enrolled at Wheaton, and am disgusted with the entire business. I don't care to study, and am avoiding the college life. What I would like is to get on the farm and work hard every day for six months until I recovered my balance.

"Honestly, Mama, I have never been so discontented and dissatisfied in my life. I know I am out of step with God but can't get out of the rut. The reason I didn't want to come back to Wheaton was because if I came I would either have to act the part of a hypocrite or suffer in reputation, the latter of which is occurring.

"Don't get the idea that it is because I am in poor physical shape. On the contrary, Dr. Jones examined me and pronounced me fit and I have been feeling fine and am out for football and getting along fine. The fact is that I am utterly sick of school, and I can't see why dropping out for a semester or even a year would ruin my life.

"If I were to catch some physical illness, to drop out would be o.k. But you would rather have me stumble along barely passing my exams, and getting nothing else out of school, merely because I am only spiritually or mentally ill.

"As it is, I suppose you will be grieved over the fact that I am not getting along well both in my school work and spiritually, however you must realize that I as well as anyone else, have ups and downs, and however deep I may go, I will be the better for the experience.

"Well, Mama, I was glad to hear that you were feeling well and I suppose you are probably very busy. Harry told me about your horseback experience and it made me admire you all the more. I hope that Papa will soon be getting home to stay with you awhile.

Lots of love, hugs, and kisses,
As ever, your loving son,
Kenneth."

There are no more letters from Kenneth to his parents until January, 1932. He either received permission or he went without it, but he spent the next four months at home. There are a few letters from this time to Harry and Grace at Wheaton, expressing his enjoyment of outdoor life and the farm animals. "The other day I was galloping Chingo hard going up the road and when we went to turn the corner hard he slipped and fell and rolled over. I thought for awhile that he was going to roll over on top of me. He cut open both knees, which made Mother mad. She says I'm too reckless on horseback. It makes the fifth time I've been thrown."

In January Strachan returned to the United States by boat, with apologies for having forgotten to bid the people in the mission hospital goodbye, and a promise to his mother to try to do better during the coming semester.

He chose all his courses with a view to their value as preparation for missionary work: physical education, including massage and diets, which he felt would be somehow useful in young people's work in Central America; Christian education, Sunday School and Church aims and methods, Synoptic Gospels, journalism, radio writing, Spanish, literature, and ornithology ("this will give me valuable background for illustrations," i.e., sermon illustrations).

His letters during these months reflect his all-consuming interest in "the work," the missionary work in which his parents were engaged and in which he hoped to participate. When his mother wrote of an impending revolution in Costa Rica he wondered how it might affect "the work." When a friend was converted, Ken saw him immediately as a prospective recruit for "the work." Every detail of life at home interested him, and he wanted to know how many were in Sunday School last week, when the peas were picked at the farm, how many students were enrolled in the institute, and whether there were any new calves. He followed his father's movements as closely as possible, praying for his preaching campaigns and encouraging the others in the family to do the same, "for that will assure his success."

Not many weeks went by before Ken began to be troubled by the fact that he was older than most of his classmates, was not yet going to graduate, and was wholly dependent on his parents' financial help. "I'm quite disgusted with myself for going to school on money I didn't earn. . . . I only wish you had a son who would give you better returns." His conscience bothered him if he missed even a week in writing home and he occasionally signed his letters "Your worthless son." In May, when only four weeks remained of the semester, he wrote what was perhaps the most distressing letter of all to his parents:

"Things have not been going very well, Mother, and I hate to tell you about it, but I know you'd rather hear it from me than elsewhere. In the first place, I want to confess that while I tried hard to get right with God on the farm that night, and thought that I had given up, I had a fight for several days after that, and in the end I lost out. Consequently I have been just as bad off as ever, perhaps worse. I signed up for the Seminary because it seemed the thing to do on the chance that things would get right before the time came. I can guess how you will be feeling when you read this. I feel like a brute—that's why I haven't told you before. My studies have, consequently, not come along so well. However, it's not that that worries me—it's the fact that I'm wasting your money and time. You speak of sending me to summer school and seminary. In times like these, I can guess what a sacrifice it must be. You have only given more and done more for me, inspite of all my wasting and backsliding, instead of putting me up against it. You can't guess how it makes me feel. It would not have been so bad if it were only that I had backslidden religiously, but I have lost any traces of manhood. I have no will power or self-control, I have not made myself do the things I know I should have done, and as a result, I am failing not only in Christian life but even more so than the most worldly man. I don't know what to do. I feel so heartily ashamed of myself when I think of what I should have done and didn't, and yet I haven't the strength or haven't gone far enough to turn back. I wonder if it isn't too late. After all your time, prayer, and expenses and hopes—I turn out like this. I don't wonder it will cut you hard. I intend to talk it over with Father when he comes, but I thought you should know first, even if it hurts you badly. Forgive me that it does.

"Harry also has not been coming along well. As my brother's keeper I have failed also, as in other things. As you know, Harry dropped school and is now doing nothing besides his work in the restaurant. He intends to go to summer school, I don't know why.

Mr. Schell has told him to finish his algebra and complete his high school work. After that I don't know what would be best for him, or me either. He dropped school for no other reason than that he got tired of it, and didn't care to go.

"I hope this letter will not be too much of a blow, though I realize that it can be nothing else. Why do you have to love us so, and expect so much of us, Mother? We're nothing but bums without any character. What is it that makes us follow along these lines? I realize how much I have hurt and wounded. I hope some day that I may turn out differently and repay you for all you have done. At present I have no confidence or self-respect. I can't promise anything, because I haven't the will power to keep it. That's how low I have fallen. . . .

"I know you must feel terribly as you read this letter—and perhaps you may derive some consolation out of the fact that I am about at the end of my rope and will be forced to turn back to the Lord, whom I have deserted so treacherously—if it isn't too late. At any rate, Mother, you can pray for me, though I don't deserve it. . . . What a despicable wretch I am to have caused any hurt.

"Please forgive me for this, Mother. I feel ashamed to meet you or Father. How anyone could go along the way I have and still love his parents I can't understand, and yet, Mother, I do love you. What a poor kind of love it has turned out to be! Please pray hard for me that I may stage a comeback.

Lots of love, your undeserving son,
Kenneth."

The semester spent in Costa Rica had made it impossible for Ken to graduate with his college class so he went on to summer school at the advice of his mother, although he wondered if "perhaps it would be a good idea for you to give me the air then I would just have to get out on my own and perhaps I'd learn to be a man." At the same time he had other ideas about what would be good for his brother. "Take him home and put him to work," was his advice to his mother. It seems that Harry was not trusted alone, either to get his schoolwork done or to take care of his own finances, and Mrs. Strachan regularly sent Harry's money to Ken, who paid his bills and allowed him the rest on installments.

The suggestion that Ken should attend seminary in the fall was not met with much enthusiasm, principally because it would be further study, and all Ken felt at this juncture was a nostalgia for the farm in the mountains of Costa Rica. "Wheaton is like the Sahara Desert for me now. Not that it has been so hot, but everything seems so dead and motionless here and because to me at present it is a place I want to get out of."

It would be bad enough to have to keep on studying. But to have to study theology was unthinkable. "I am not in a right spiritual state. . . . A change in environment does not mean a change of heart." He had discussed the idea with a faculty member at Wheaton and been strongly warned against it on the ground that it would be dangerous and hypocritical to take up the ministry of the Gospel in such a state. "All would be settled were I to come to a definite surrender, and I wish that would happen, but I don't know when." Somehow he expected to be moved upon, to be cornered. The "definite surrender" he saw not as an act of will, but as something that would "happen" to him from the outside, and if it did not happen, there was very little he could do. But then, on second thought, maybe there was something—maybe he should simply *make* himself decide. But no, "guess I'm not strong enough to make myself come to a definite decision," he told his mother. "I don't know just how to express it, Mama, but I'm afraid I'm getting to the stage of positive unbelief. And yet I believe in Christianity but every time I think of it in a personal way I have a skeptic feeling which makes me wonder what's the use. What I need is a good jolt to wake me up and I'm afraid that I'm going to get it if things go on this way much longer."

Things went on. The summer was a "fast one," Ken wrote several months later to his sister Grace, who was at home with her parents. "I went with one of the prettiest girls in the neighborhood. She was a wonderful dancer, dressed beautifully, sang well, extremely popular with mobs of fellows. Every dance we went to people would pick her out. Dancing, drinking, smoking, bridge, plenty of cars, always something doing, and with a girl like that. Do you think I was happy? The only thing the summer's experience did for me was make me respect in a new light the fellow that plodded on and kept his responsibilities. I still like to dance, go to shows, maybe smoke, and I haven't said or determined not to, for me they are sin, and perhaps I'll fall lots of times, Gracie, but one thing I'm holding on to—Jesus has saved me, from my sins, from the *power* of sin and from the *consequences* of sin. Sometimes I feel terribly worldly, want to tear out, but through it all, I know I'm saved. Saved from what? First from eternal condemnation, which, however much you may try to forget it, is a fact. Secondly, saved from a rotten life here on earth. My new relation with God wasn't an emotional one. I didn't renounce the world and expect a flood of blessing. I just said, 'O God, I like worldly pleasures and I'm weak enough to fall lots of times, but I believe.' "

The choice Ken made set the rudder for the rest of his life. He still had not achieved his college degree, he knew that he was far from "spiritually qualified" to enter theological seminary, he had no natural inclination toward Christian service, but when his father visited the two boys in Wheaton at the end of the summer and expressed his hope that Ken would go to the Evangelical Theological College in Dallas, the decision was made. "It's hell to go on this way," he told Harry. There had to be a different way, and it was not difficult to decide that the way his parents had gone, the way they hoped he would go, was for him God's way, and seminary was the first step.

CHAPTER 4

The Evangelical Theological College was eight years old when Strachan enrolled there. It had been founded to defend "Dispensational" or Scofieldian theology, and it had sixty students, nearly all from Fundamentalist homes where other seminaries were regarded as modernistic or heretical. The college was housed in a single neo-Spanish-style building near the center of Dallas, at that time a city of twenty-five thousand.

The institution was aptly named, and the courses Ken took provided a heavy dose of evangelical theology—ten subjects, all related to preaching or Bible study, including one course called "Realization of Spiritual Life." There were no courses in liberal arts or sciences, and the twelve-thousand-volume library consisted almost exclusively of reference works on theology. The degrees offered were Bachelor of Theology and Master of Theology. Dr. Lewis Sperry Chafer, president of the college, Ken described as "a small man, about my size, yet he has an air of poise and inward dignity which makes him seem much larger." His courses enthralled Ken, who began to realize that Christianity was more than just saying one's prayers.

There was in Kenneth Strachan, who could be so deeply pessimistic about himself, an almost airy optimism about other people and situations, an offhand assurance that "things would work out." He was in Dallas during the Depression, and the administrators of the school seriously wondered if it might be necessary to close. Ken informed his parents that things looked pretty bad, but he had "no fear whatever of their having to close the school." One of his professors he described as boring, but hastened to add cheerfully, "It's

25

early yet, and he may become more interesting as he goes along." He admitted enjoying his studies, but was hesitant to hope that this would last. As in Wheaton days, descriptions of events seldom went beyond a "fair" time, and anticipation of a dinner engagement was cautious: "Guess we ought to have a fairly enjoyable time if we don't eat too much."

By comparison with letters from Wheaton, however, Ken's letters from Dallas indicate a general sense of what may almost be called well-being. For one thing, his financial situation, although still tightly controlled by his mother, did not press daily upon his conscience because some of his bills were paid by the semester. He wrote that it was a satisfaction to be able for the first time in seven years to eat regularly without having to wonder what the bill would be. He had, of course, found it necessary to break the news gently to his mother, at the beginning of the school year, that he would need $30.50 for a suit, and money for a topcoat, one pair of shoes, a trunk, and some socks and ties—a total of $71, which he hoped would not be too big a blow, but if it should be, he offered to drop out of school and work.

He was impressed by the hospitality and courtesy of the South. To his brother—not to his mother—he confided that there were "more good-looking women than I've ever seen before. I wonder if it's characteristic of the South? L.B. is here, going to S.M.U. I'm not bragging, but I think she's got her eye on me. I sure hate it. Every time I go to the Scofield Church I have to dodge her all the time. As a result I don't go over there very often although it's got a nice bunch of kids there."

To his mother he described the young people of another church as "very worldy Christians, but they're all that way down here." The church he called "a bit modernistic," and this perhaps spurred him to agree to teach a Sunday School class of "tough kids" of twelve years of age, with whom he succeeded in holding attention. This triumph he related to his mother as "an awfully big thrill." His outrage over an incident that took place one Sunday morning shows his lifelong disgust with superficiality. "The pastor came to my class to give a special talk on salvation. After speaking to those twelve-year-olds for about twenty minutes on such subjects as the foreknowledge of God, His plan of salvation, the sealing of the Holy Spirit, Sin, etc., in language which I doubt an average crowd of adults would comprehend, he asked how many were saved. All but one raised their hands. He picked on this one and fired a lot of questions at the scared kid, who mumbled, 'Yes, sir,' to all of them, shook hands with him, and later in the church service the pastor spoke of the wonderful conversion which he had wrought in Sunday School. It made me so sick that I almost felt like dropping the whole business. Mother, I'm convinced that it is because of such brainless, self-righteous fools that the churches of today are loaded with Christians who have not grasped Life Eternal. That kid was no more saved than the devil himself. Don't you think it's rotten?"

During the preceding summer at Wheaton Ken had worked at a swimming pool and perfected his diving technique. Swimming and diving became his passion, and he thought it extremely important to keep in shape physically, so he joined the YMCA of Dallas and soon conceived the idea of combining his need for exercise with his desire to serve the Lord. He started a swimming club for boys which brought him great enjoyment and led him to hope that some day in Costa Rica he might build a pool at the farm and use this means to attract boys to a Bible camp.

In addition to his two weekly boys' classes, he tried preaching on the street, but found himself "as self-conscious as a bashful boy. I'll never be much of a speaker," he told his mother. "Don't have the voice or the ability to express things clearly." But he saw needs all around him, and attempted, sometimes blunderingly, to meet those needs. "Don't forget me in prayer, Mother. I need all the ballast I can get."

There was a clearer sense of direction in Ken's life by this time. He had opted for a missionary career, and set about methodically preparing himself for it. His grades were in the high eighties and nineties for the first semester. He still, however, entertained no illusions about his personal fitness for this role, and acknowledged in a letter home, "Frankly, the thought of spending eternity in a saintly ethereal form, twanging a harp, has little appeal to me. However, I believe it will be much more than that, but how and in what form?"

After a Christmas vacation spent at the school ("My doings weren't very exciting but what was most important, I was doing something most of the time and so didn't have much time to wish for a better vacation") Ken wrote on New Year's Day, "If I were a bit more courageous I would take Philippians 3:13, 14 ['I count not myself to have apprehended: but this one thing I do, forgetting those things which are behind, and reaching forth unto those things which are before, I press toward the mark for the prize of the high calling of God in Christ Jesus'] and make them my testimony, but I have become rather a coward, preferring to sneak along quietly, hoping the Devil will overlook me and not tempt me too much. Worldly pleasures have a terrible drawing power, especially in these days but I'm beginning to realize one can choose one's battlefield . . . but it's hard, and not a life of blissful hymn-chanting."

His letter to Harry on January 3, 1933, was in a different vein. "Well, here we're starting another year, Harry, pretty soon we'll be old, I with a big pot and you with a big family (perhaps). The other night I couldn't sleep so just for fun went back remembering all the things we'd done. It only seems such a short time since we crossed the Andes in the little train and I made you cut your tongue. Do you remember the boat trip up and those few months in Ridgefield Park, going to grade school, and then the year out in Kansas City—the time spent in Johnstown, the summer up at the lake and all the games we used to play? Then the trip to Costa Rica and living in Jimenez' house, going to Escuela Metodista, being on Boy Scout troop and serving with them during the earthquake—seeing the Institute building going up, taking those hikes with Freddy out into the country—going up to the farm in Esparta—to Puntarenas—then coming up to the States to school—and seven years at Wheaton for me, four for you. And now in a few years we may both be back in Costa Rica. Gosh, I hate to realize that time has gone by so quickly, don't you?"

There is a significant difference between the letters he wrote to his brother and those to his sister. To Harry, Ken was always just a buddy, a pal who never grew up. He did on rare occasions chide Harry in a mild way—perhaps because he felt it his duty to help his mother in this manner—but usually his attitude was offhand and breezy. To Grace, however, he wrote letters that reveal a deep personal concern for her. He wanted to help her make decisions, he wrote often trying to cheer her up or encourage her in her Christian life, though his expression was not a preachy one. He was proud that she was his sister—proud of her as a woman, proud of her ambition to become a doctor, proud of her beauty and dignity, horrified if he ever detected a spot on her dress, anxious to defend her to his parents whenever they worried about their daughter's behavior. He loved her. He seemed freer with her than with anyone else. With his parents he was excessively afraid of offending or of appearing independent. With Harry he was restrained because he felt inferior—Harry was taller, more skilled in athletics, more popular, more courageous to be himself. Grace, however, was his friend, with whom he could be most completely himself, and for this reason it is possible to discern in his letters to her the slow process of maturing which is nearly imperceptible in other letters. Just a week after writing the letter above to Harry, Ken wrote to Grace, "I appreciate your confiding in me how you feel, as I can well understand it and know more or less just how you feel.

"It certainly puts one in a muddle to try and figure what's right and what isn't and to fix for oneself certain rules for behavior. Everything nowadays tends so much to the belief of living merrily today for tomorrow we die—that I don't blame you for wondering just what to think. And as with me, I know that the sanctimonious expression of 'My Jesus, I love Thee' (no sacrilege meant) doesn't help you out anymore than the other because you don't feel in a mood of loving anybody much less singing about it. On the one hand you have a worldly life which your bringing up makes you realize won't do and on the other hand, Christianity seems to be too extreme and somehow not a bit attractive. But after all, Gracie, it's the only thing that works. Christianity is not a religion demanding blind faith . . . not a psychological fraud, man-invented. Not that a mental belief will make any difference in your condition, but it will show you that it is not an illogical, unfounded belief. As for H. and his semi-pantheistic philosophy—however much he may talk about it, it doesn't work, and as for his arguments, you can find a hundred holes in them. A refusal of personal responsibility and self-indulgence in pleasures is a philosophy which reason alone, apart from any religious convictions, tells you will never work out nor bring happiness. Our reason tells us that but in spite of it we want to go on and find out for ourselves. Well, I found out this past summer. . . .

"I don't expect life to be a bed of roses, but the best way to keep from being in a mental torture all the while is to forget about yourself, make yourself think of others and you'll find it easier to enjoy life. Boy, I did plenty of mental sweating when I came here. You'll always be unhappy and dissatisfied as long as you sit and think about how rotten things are and how much you would like to be on board ship or someplace dancing, etc. It's all baloney. It's hard to appreciate the importance of eternity or feel repentant for your sins, but you don't have to—just try Christ's recipe for everyday happiness and contentment just for your own private self, without any testifying, etc. and see how it works out. If you don't make a lot of noise about it but just settle it in your heart and let it work out in your life, you'll notice the difference, Gracie. The only reason I took it was because it was the last alternative. I tried everything else (actually) and in my heart of hearts I know it was the right thing.

"Well, Gracie, forgive my preaching to you—but I hope you settle things, not so another soul will be won for the kingdom, but so that you'll find the true road to happiness.

"With regard to the boys you mentioned. I just don't know what to say, Gracie. While in the ideal there should be a perfect and beautiful relation between the spiritual and the physical, in actual life there isn't, and sometimes the discovery of that is shocking. Everywhere is sex stressed and advertised so it's no wonder you run up against a lot of that stuff, but if you keep away from it, Gracie, I know in the end you'll be glad of it—especially when you meet the man you'll love. We're all human and there's nothing especially beautiful about human nature.

"Lots of love, Gracie. I hope I haven't been too serious or heavy.
Your brother, Kenneth."

With Grace he shared his new love for poetry. Kipling had captured his imagination and he told his sister she must read "The Ballad of East and West," "Tomlinson," "Mandalay," and the "Recessional." Robert Service appealed to him for the same reasons

Kipling did—a "rough, outdoor style, far better than pretty thoughts of flowers and nature common to so many English poets." He must also have read Edna St. Vincent Millay, for he wrote to Grace, "I know that the 'pretty light' of burning candles at both ends does not pay for the burnt ends no matter how beautiful the light may look and yet to go through life with one's candle conservatively and properly lit seems drab and uninteresting, and it likely is, except for the hope of something better which every man has hid in his heart, but which is given to some only to realize and the realization of that is, I think, the greatest experience that one can have in his life."

There was another experience besides that of committing oneself to God which Ken was looking for, and again it was Grace in whom he confided. "I have an important question to ask you, Gracie. Are there still any young women of beautiful appearance and gracious personality and developed character with which a young man might get acquainted? I hope you'll be able to tell me where. Please don't get the idea that I'm feverishly hunting around but you know I wouldn't mind meeting any which might conform to the above. It seems to me that they are mighty scarce. (I'm glad my sister fills the bill.) Well, I hope you'll be able to give me a lot of good advice on this point, and how to proceed, etc. etc."

He still wrote very faithfully and affectionately to his mother. After reading an article she had written in the mission paper, the *Evangelist,* he told her he had felt like running up to her room and giving her a big hug and lots of "slobbery kisses." When he learned that she was considering introducing the raising of hogs at the farm, he warned, "You'd better have a three-months' prayer meeting to arrange with God the matter of wind." When she wondered if he had yet met anyone he might consider as a wife he answered, "There's only two persons that fill my ideal so far—you and Gracie. . . . However, you are my sweetheart yet and so far I'm not interested in any other." When his studies took him into the area of "false cults" it was his mother's rather than his father's opinion that he sought. She was alert to world news, and he often consulted her about what she thought was going to happen. Father was still traveling far and wide throughout the Americas, and seldom figures in the correspondence between mother and son. When Ken learned that his father was expected home he eagerly awaited details of the reunion, although he jokingly conceded that his mother would probably "be sorry to have to take care of his ties and clothes once more." It seemed a "funny thing" that her next letter made hardly any mention at all of his father's arrival. Ken and a missionary friend were discussing Mr. and Mrs. Strachan on one occasion, and decided that she was clearly the better public speaker. Ken felt keenly his own inferiority to either of his parents, and it was not helped when he and his father were invited to speak on the same platform. Ken gave a personal testimony concerning what Christ meant to him, and his father criticized him severely afterward for not putting enough "background and pep" into the talk. "He's right," Ken wrote, "but I don't like testimonies anyway, for the large share of them are not consistent with the life behind it."

Later in the spring Ken cautiously let his mother know that things were better than they had been for a long time. "Have decided never to talk about my spiritual condition because when I do I always have a let-down, and my tendency is to be very unstable. But I have wanted to tell you oftentimes how much nearer and dearer Jesus is becoming to me."

He had written to Harry about the past summer's work in Wheaton, saying that he did not want to spend another one like it. "It's some fun but doesn't lead anywhere, and it's plenty easy for me to do, so I have to keep away." He found a place with fewer temptations—a children's Bible camp in Manitoba. Here, too, he was gratified with a sense of worthwhile deeds accomplished, but at the same time questioning his qualifications for "full-time" service. He even went so far as to wonder if his mother, who seemed to him infallible, had ever had a moment of doubt. "How do you feel about things, Mother? Has Christian work ever been a bit of a strain to you? Sometimes I wonder whether the ministry is really the place for me. I am too cynical and critical. I'm glad of one thing, however—I no longer have doubts as to whether Christianity is a huge hoax."

CHAPTER 5

Several times during his Wheaton years Ken had referred to his need of a jolt of some kind to bring him to terms with reality and with Christ. Precisely what sort of jolt he expected he would probably not have known if asked. But then, by definition, a jolt is a surprise. He had finished the first year at seminary and a month of his second year when it came.

His brother had enrolled in an agricultural course in the University of Florida with a view to assisting in the work of the farm in Costa Rica. For some time he had not been well, and had written during the summer of a stubborn crop of boils which kept him inactive. His freshman year had begun and he was still feeling fatigued and depressed when a hurricane struck the campus of the university, and Harry, along with other students, helped in rescue work and clearing the debris. He contracted malaria, was put in the hospital, and, probably because he was physically below par, did not respond to treatment. His father, who was then traveling in the United States, received word of his condition from Harry's fraternity, and notified Ken. Ken's letter to his mother reveals again his ability to hope where others were concerned.

"The past week or two must have been an awful strain on you, Mother, and I'm so sorry that it has. The thought of Harry in critical condition has just made me feel rotten. He always gets the tough breaks. It was a comfort after receiving Father's telegram telling of the seriousness of his illness, to know that I could fall back on the Comforter, but somehow or other I couldn't help imagining what might happen and it made me feel terribly blue. He's such a swell kid. I'm sure that someday the three of us will be back there with you and Father and how nice it will be to be helping you out with the work. Did you notice the Keswick calendar verses for Saturday and Sunday? Proverbs 3:5 and II Corinthians 12:9." The verses were, "Trust in the Lord with all thine heart and lean not unto thine own understanding," and "My grace is sufficient for thee, for my strength is made perfect in weakness." Ken's letter closed with, "I hope that by the time you receive this Harry will be well on the road to recovery. Right now I wish I were in his shoes.

"Lots of love, Mother dear, and I wish I could say just what I want to say but it's hard to say it without sounding mushy."

The fraternity sent Mr. Strachan a second message indicating that Harry had improved, and a third saying that he had had a relapse and his condition was critical. When they heard this both father and brother went to Florida to see Harry in the hospital. Ken never told what passed between them during his time alone with his brother, but he did tell of walking the streets of the city that night and praying as he had never prayed in his life that God would have mercy, that Harry would not die. During the early hours of the morning he felt assured that his prayer had been heard. It had been a jolt, and a bad one, but he thanked God that it was not going to be any worse.

Mrs. Strachan and Grace were on their way from Costa Rica by boat, and Ken went to Miami to meet them. While he was there a telegram came. It said that Harry had died. He had had an allergic reaction to the drug administered for malaria.

There was nothing for his mother and sister to do but to return home. His father had other commitments, and, with characteristic conviction that nothing must interfere with these, which were to him the Lord's work, left Ken to make arrangements for the body to be transported to Costa Rica.

It was, both before and after it happened, unthinkable. For the rest of his life Ken found it almost impossible to refer to his brother's death, and of his own deep remorse because of it he could not speak at all. Harry, the kid brother who always made his own way in life, who was favored by his mother because she could understand him, who endeared people to him without the effort that Ken's friendships cost him—this Harry was now dead. And the God who had brought Ken back to Himself so recently and had proved His faithfulness in forgiving and restoring him, the God who had comforted him and his parents when the word came of Harry's sickness, the God who commands trust and promises grace, the God to whom Ken prayed that night as he walked through the city—this God had let Harry die.

In his desperation Ken tried to mollify with words the real significance of the event. Perhaps he could make it over into something other than an utter calamity.

"I went over to the undertaker's yesterday and he was very nice. . . . While there I spent an hour alone with Harry in the chapel and while there the thought came to me that he and I were returning home together. So, Mother, it will not be a sad home-coming but a sweet one, and we'll have Harry with us all the time. I couldn't help remembering the past years and little events and incidents and though such memories are sad yet we'll have them with us to remember him until the day comes when we'll all be together again, and that time is not far off.

"Lots of love, Mother dear. We'll soon be with you."

There is no record of Ken's thoughts or feelings during the year which followed. He accompanied the body to his home and stayed until the following September (1934). Whether his faith was so badly shaken that he had no incentive to pursue the Way of the Cross which he had chosen, or whether he deliberately set out to challenge the God who had let him down, there is no way of knowing. It is said that he and his sister behaved so badly during that year that their parents obliged them to make public confession in the church of their misdeeds. One of Ken's first letters to his mother the next year acknowledged that he had failed her again, that he had promised to be to her two sons but was selfish and complaining, had indeed "failed in everything a son should be to his mother." He could not ask her forgiveness because his heart, he said, was hard, "but I do love you, Mother."

CHAPTER 6

Two more years remained for Ken at seminary, years when he took seriously the necessity of preparing himself in study for the work of the mission, but when he continued to feel that his spiritual state was a very precarious one. The ability to enjoy a cigarette or a movie—things not forbidden by the seminary as they had been at Wheaton, the emphasis at Dallas being on "grace" rather than "law" —Ken equated with spiritual coldness or backsliding, trying to tell himself on the one hand that he was "free" to behave as he liked, and being severely pricked in his conscience on the other because, as he had told Grace, of such things as smoking, movies, and dancing, "for me it is sin." He read *Hudson Taylor's Spiritual Secret* and wrote to his mother that it "sure makes you feel small." When he read *Ambassadors for Christ* his comment was, "Guess I don't belong." Later he said, "I am totally unfit for the Lord's service." Nevertheless he was convinced that he had no choice but the Lord's service. "I don't know the Lord's will on the matter, but my own heart and mind are settled (if He will only keep me)" he wrote on April, 1935. "I feel definitely now that He wants me in Christian service. God's grace is very evident to me . . . due to your prayers. Please don't say anything about it because I've slipped so many times that I'm not sure of myself, but I have come to get an idea of God's grace and it's wonderful."

His eagerness to be in Costa Rica is evidenced again and again in his letters when he writes, "only one more year!" or "I'd give anything to be there now!"

He did a great deal of thinking about the problems of the mission

36

field and found himself involved almost before he knew it. Sharing the platform of a small country church with a fellow student one evening he was placed in the awkward position of competing for interest for his own mission versus another work which the student was representing. This went against the grain for Ken, and he refused to enter the competition, speaking instead on the general need of mission work in Latin America. When he observed, on another occasion, two well-known evangelical leaders asking for large offerings "to cover expenses" of their meetings Ken was outraged. "They themselves should not do the asking," he told his mother. He had misgivings, too, about the financial position of his parents' mission. They called it a "faith" mission, which Ken was told meant that it depended on God alone for financial support. "Denominational" missions, far larger and better known, were supported by the pledges and offerings of the membership. "My question is this, Mother," he wrote. "If we're a faith mission ought we to put our needs before man and depend on man to that extent?"

He had apparently criticized his mother's generosity while he was at home, and wrote from Dallas to say, "Do you remember how opposed I was to being too kind to people as they took advantage of it? I am changing my idea on that. After all, there are precious few breaks for them in this world at that."

His mother had experimented with employing Latin Americans as missionaries, and had given up the idea because she did not believe they were trustworthy. Ken, with an unusual prophetic understanding of the trend mission work would take, wrote, "In spite of the fact that you have lost faith in native workers, it seems to me that in the days to come you will be more and more dependent on them." The next thirty years of the mission's history demonstrated how right he was.

There existed a misunderstanding between the LAEC and another faith mission also engaged in work in Costa Rica. There had been several attempts to mend matters, but each side felt the other was to blame. Mrs. Strachan wrote to her son that he would do well to say nothing at the seminary of the difficulties that existed. "Their work is about on the rocks, torn to pieces by dissension. . . . Yesterday Mr. H. came to see me to ask if we could again have united prayer meetings. I told him flatly no, that we were trying to build up and consolidate our work and that the fruit of our cooperation in united services in the past was a movement which disrupted the Templo congregation. Their congregation is certainly reaping what they sowed, and it should be a great lesson to the people and to the workers."

At a later date things were patched up to a degree, "for their good," in Mrs. Strachan's opinion. "No," contradicted Ken, "for ours." He saw already the necessity of working in harmony with others who profess the same Gospel, and believed that his association with fellow students who were planning to go to Latin America might later lead to the cementing of friendships with other mission boards. This idea in itself must have been a bombshell to his mother, who had never found it necessary to work in any situation of which she was not in charge.

One other piece of advice which Ken offered to his mother was that she make it a policy never to accept any single women for the mission, for the simple reason that "there's always trouble." It appears that this argument did not convince her, but her replies were always affectionate, goodhumored, and domineering. She was as absent-minded as ever, forgetting to send him things he asked for, addressing a letter to him at Wheaton when he was at Dallas, neglecting to mention whether she had ever received the money Ken had sent to buy flowers for Harry's grave. Ken continued to depend on her to make his decisions, though there is evidence that this was bothering him increasingly. He still wanted to get his bachelor's degree from Wheaton, and would have to attend summer school in order to do it, but the big question was of course money, and there was no source from which to expect it aside from his parents. He once expressed the opinion that it would perhaps be better for him not to accept any help at all from them for summer school, and when he received no comment, either veto or endorsement, on this suggestion, he remained "indefinite as to what I should do. It would be sort of weak to fall back on you." In the same letter he hastens to assure his mother that he is not getting independent, in case she should suppose he were. "I have felt more than ever before the debt I owe you both and it is not my slightest thought to cut myself off from you." But then—what to do about school? It was a nice question. "I do want to do His will, but what is it? To accept money from you and go to summer school, or not to? What do you think?" His understanding of the will of God was nearly indistinguishable, in this area at least, from the will of his parents. "Write by return airmail and give me your advice or decision. I am perfectly willing to do either." He received a cable: REGISTER AT WHEATON.

This time he studied. He made straight A's and got his A.B. degree at the age of twenty-five.

Whether his college graduation jolted his mother to the realization that her boy was now a man, or whether it was the frightening prospect of his joining the mission still a bachelor is not indicated in her letters, but it was on his twenty-fifth birthday, and again and again during the year that followed, that she wrote, suggesting it was time he thought about the serious business of finding a wife. "That is of all others the most important thing ahead of you, so we will be praying about it. I hope you yourself pray about it sometimes." Come to think of it, he hadn't, actually, Ken acknowledged, but would certainly begin now.

Between his graduation from Wheaton and his returning to Dallas for his final year, Ken paid a visit to Keswick, New Jersey, with his sister and his father. A new appreciation for them both developed, and he wrote to his father to apologize for the critical spirit he had formerly had, and to say that he was "grateful to God for allowing me to know you better. I have always felt sort of separate, but realize it has always been my own imagination."

His feeling "sort of separate" was certainly more than imagination, since he had never spent a prolonged period with his father. Evangelistic journeys had taken Mr. Strachan away from home during as much of Ken's life as he could remember, and the hasty stopovers in Wheaton hardly compensated, even though his father often did something special for his children such as taking them to a tennis match or an ice hockey game. Both parent and child made as much of such special events as possible, but neither seemed to be aware of the fearful price being paid—or if, possibly, the father reckoned on it, it was not, as he saw it, more than ought legitimately to be paid by a servant of the Lord or by his children. Had not Jesus

Himself said, "If any man come to me, and hate not his father, and mother, and wife, and children, and brethren, and sisters, yea, and his own life also, he cannot be my disciple"?

Ken revered his father, who was a somewhat legendary hero to him, but it could hardly be said that he shared much intimacy with him.

To Grace he wrote, "Gracie dear, Here I am back in my room just after you and Father have gone, and feeling like a cloud-burst. Please forgive me if I hurt your feelings. . . . Sorry I seem so cold about things but really inside, Gracie, I was feeling plenty. . . . When I think what you are my eyes get bleary. I know from things that have dropped that you think pretty highly of me but don't get taken in by superficialities—athletic ability, etc. is inherited, no credit to me, surface stuff anyway. What really counts is the character and guts beneath, and you have them, I don't.

"Thank you for the money. At first I thought I would save it and put it away as a reminder . . . but now I feel that perhaps the best thing to do would be to get something special with it. . . . We could give it to the Lord from both of us, for something special, after much thought. Tell me what it shall be.

"I have criticized a lot during the time here but I have loved the time together and now that it is over I feel like a cry baby. Like a rat, too, for being critical of little things instead of recognizing what a real man I have for a father, and what a real 'man' I have for a sister. . . .

"Much love, Gracie, may God be near you, keeping and blessing.
Your brother, Kenneth."

To his father on the same day he wrote, "All summer I've been realizing how wonderful Gracie is but I realize it more than ever now. Can't tell you how deeply she touched my heart this morning. Don't know what to say about it." He told his mother that Grace was "so much superior to me in every way. Someday I feel that she will have a big name. . . . She has a lot of stuff in her. I expect her to be a great woman."

His travels during the summer yielded no prospects in answer to his prayers for a wife, and back Ken went to Dallas where possibilities were decidedly limited. By midyear, even his father began to worry, and wrote that it might be well to find a good wife. His mother, as though this were her initial mention of the subject, wrote, "Kenneth, you should pray much about a life companion, a single man is not half so useful or *safe* (you know how the silly girls run after a boy) as a married man, and if you once come down there's little chance of getting the right girl here. Think and pray about it, son, as I am doing for you."

What had hardly seemed cause for concern became a knotty problem to Kenneth Strachan, and his unrest was apparent in his letters. "I wish I had time to write you more at length, son of mine," wrote his mother, "because I fear you are carrying a burden about your 'problems' although you do not say much about what they are. I hope you are not feeling bad about what I said about finding a wife. Don't take it that you have to marry whether you like it or not, and don't on any account propose to a girl unless you really feel she's the only girl in the world for you. It would be taking an awful chance to do otherwise and don't you do it. I feel sure the Lord has the girl for you somewhere and that in His time you will meet her, but don't carry any burden about the matter."

Ken's faith had reached a new intricacy when he was able to write, "Don't worry about what I shall do. It will, Lord willing, be what the Lord's will is."

He had begun to include a Scripture reference at the end of almost every letter to his mother, a practice perhaps highly thought of at the seminary. Oddly enough, however, the commonest religious exercise in Christian America, Sunday morning church attendance, did not seem to hold any special importance in Ken's view of things, nor was he even reluctant to mention this to his parents, who were strict observers of the Sabbath. "Generally I do not attend Sunday morning church. I find it more profitable to rest."

Sunday evenings sometimes found him attending country church services. One of these was a Pentecostal church, which he described as "a most peculiar form of worship, although I think some of them were saved. Their music was all jazz, including a set of tap drums, tambourine, sax, trumpet, and banjos. They sang Negro hymns to a dance-hall rhythm of low order. The preacher spoke many real truths in his Negro way. I enjoyed it, and not only from the viewpoint of a bystander."

Once he went to a Negro church where the minister was a woman.

She was expounding the seven *dispensations* of the Bible. It was a big word, and it ruffled her each time she came to it, but she managed it well until the fourth, when it escaped her altogether. "And now we come to the fourth" (here, according to Ken's description, she swallowed hard, trying to remember) "to the fourth—to the fourth predicament." Ken found himself having to stuff his mouth with a handkerchief in order not to burst out laughing.

Strachan had made his decision to join the LAEC. His career was settled. There remained yet the *when* and *how*, and for these decisions he looked again to his mother. "What are your plans concerning me when I graduate?" he asked. She replied that he must make formal application to the home council of the mission. Ken wrote back, "I am awaiting orders, however, I earnestly hope you'll forget any relationship except that of worker to the council. The one thing that bothers me is the idea that you still regard me as in the nest. However, I'd appreciate knowing what you want me to do."

He was terribly eager to go to Costa Rica immediately after graduation from seminary, but Mother Strachan vetoed that idea since the Bible Institute in San José would be in midsession at that time, and neither she nor he liked the prospect of his beginning his missionary career doing "odd jobs" for other missionaries.

Ken took inventory of his qualifications for the task ahead and found himself still wanting. He dreamed that he was teaching, and was completely at a loss for Spanish words. He wrote that he wished that he could get some music into his "thick skull" but simply could not understand it. He regretted his dislike of people—it would be pleasant, as a missionary, to be able to say that one liked people. "I think I like dogs better than people," he admitted.

He graduated *cum laude* from the Evangelical Theological College of Dallas in May, 1936, with a Bachelor of Theology degree.

CHAPTER 7

Having safely established his position as a bona-fide member of the LAEC, R. Kenneth Strachan, missionary, came as close to appearing independent as he had ever done. He wrote to his father, "I want to definitely insist that you leave it up to me entirely to make my own plans for the summer if you do not need me in Costa Rica. I know you would feel the same way if you were in my shoes." It took some doing to make sure that he was not needed, and, his mother having failed to give a reply, Ken wrote to ask his father what his mother wanted. At last he was told definitely to remain in the States following seminary graduation, so the summer was spent doing pastoral work in Houston, Texas, with a fellow graduate, Wilton Nelson, who was also an LAEC candidate.

Then followed an exchange of correspondence regarding travel arrangements—Father suggested he come south via Cuba, Ken wrote to ask his mother if this would be all right. He went to New York to embark on a ship, entertaining a forlorn and desperate hope: "possibly I'll find the girl up there that the Lord has for me." His mother by this time was not so desperate as he, for one afternoon as she was lying in a hammock at siesta time she found herself complaining to God because He had so far not answered her prayers that her son would find a wife. His answer was clear and reassuring: I have that all taken care of.

Ken's arrival in Costa Rica marked the beginning of his taking things—at least a few things—into his own hands. He had decided before he sailed that he needed two things. One was responsibility. Accordingly, and over the protests of his mother, he moved into one of the Institute dormitories instead of into his parents' apartment as they had planned. Having studied a recent photograph of himself he decided that the other thing he needed was maturity—the picture made him wonder if he would ever grow up—and the only immediately effective measure to be taken toward this end was to grow a moustache, which he did, also to the surprise of his parents.

The Institute was housed in one of the original buildings built by Mrs. Strachan in the early days of their settling in San José. It was a solid square structure set flush with the sidewalk of a wide, now paved street in the southern part of town. A set of double wooden doors in the thick adobe walls opened into a patio or courtyard around which were rooms used for classes, living quarters, and offices. The "Annex" where Ken established himself was a two-story frame building with an inner patio surrounded by rooms. He ate in the dining room with other missionaries and students.

Ken was not certain of his ability to speak Spanish. He had been too many years away from the sound of it. He knew that to be a good missionary he must learn it, and zealously set about taking formal lessons. Within a few months he had mastered it. Acting as dean and teaching classes in the Institute were his initiation into "the work." He joined his mother (and father, if he happened to be at home) in her inflexible custom of afternoon tea, and these were occasions when mother and son became acquainted as they had not been before, and at times their similar natures clashed. There were some heated debates over the tea table on theology, missionary methodology, and subjects of a more immediate and personal nature. Where Susan Strachan had been a veritable Queen Victoria in her domain—for her husband had deliberately, as has been seen, left nearly all responsibility for the management of the San José work in her hands—she now found that there was another voice, uncomfortably like her own in certainty and vehemence, to be listened to. Not that Ken was in a position to influence policies at this early stage—he was a rookie, and gracefully accepted his position—but he could not refrain from airing his opinions, some of which had been carefully thought out during college and seminary years, and which eventually shaped policies under his later administration. His mother, on her part, had a sense of humor and an earthiness which balanced her powerful will and strictness, and she was able to hear her son out with surprising equanimity. For one of her generation to do this was extraordinary. She acknowledged the existence of shifting patterns in mission work in other parts of the world, and the necessity of considering world affairs in their influence on missionary strategy. Her mind was far from a closed one. She had always made it a practice to read daily newspapers and a certain number of books. In spite of her strong conviction that the Lord had entrusted the work of the LAEC into her hands she never regarded it as solely *her* work. She tried hard not to grind her own ax, and even felt that the time might conceivably come when the mission need no longer exist. The introduction of the younger men's somewhat revolutionary concepts led the mission into a period of transition and groping.

At Thanksgiving Mrs. Strachan had gone to considerable trouble to procure a turkey for the mission "family," as the missionaries called themselves. The students, on the other hand, were given chicken, no doubt because Thanksgiving had no particular meaning to them as a holiday, and chicken was perfectly acceptable. Shortly afterward Kenneth gave a talk entitled "Chicken for the Students, Turkey for the Missionaries." There is no record of the effect this bombshell had on his mother, but it may be assumed that it did not pass unnoticed.

Mother and son alike were loved by the students, although Ken winced at some of her dealings with them. He found her one day berating a student for not mopping the patio properly, and ten minutes later she was laughing heartily with the same student. Ken himself could "blow hot and cold" as she did. Once he found his students in church history class ill-prepared, and marched out of the classroom in high dudgeon, only to apologize to them in the next session.

Ken looked for avenues of service besides classwork and counseling. He sent groups of students out to "evangelize" small towns in the area—to knock on doors, hand out leaflets or Scripture portions, to hold brief meetings on the streets, to accost individuals with a view to informing as many as possible of their sinful state and the remedy provided by Christ the Son of God. When he himself took a morning off to go swimming he and his Costa Rican companion "evangelized the caretakers and attendants before going into the pool." He began to wonder what were the fruits of the Bible training which his parents had been giving for so many years, and on a trip to Guatemala tried to round up as many of the Institute alumni as possible. Rodolfo Cruz, a graduate of the Class of '33, was a pastor in Guatemala, and remembers a long talk with Ken, sitting in a park and walking the streets, when Ken spoke earnestly of his hopes for the future of the mission and of the students who had attended the Institute. "He spoke as if he had had much experience of the difficulties and the price to be paid in the Lord's work," said Rodolfo, "but I knew he had not had much. He spoke lovingly and earnestly. For me, it was a beautiful afternoon." Years later, Cruz himself joined the mission.

During a vacation from seminary duties Ken made a trip into the interior lowlands with a Costa Rican named Hernán, in order to evangelize a seldom-reached area. Here, for perhaps the first time in his life, he felt free and happy and useful. This was missionary work as he had envisioned it, "pioneer" work at the grass roots. He was cut off from communication with his parents, at liberty to become once more a *Tico* (the term Costa Ricans used for themselves, in contrast to *Macho*, the name used for foreigners).

Wearing sombreros and cowboy chaps, short boots with spurs and no shirts if it was hot, the two men rode horseback by day, swapping stories and smoking cigarettes to pass the time. There was some hard traveling through heavy jungle where they saw monkeys, beautiful birds, and strange creatures like the armadillo. Sometimes the trail would lead over wide plains filled with fruit trees or through grasslands. Sometimes it crossed a jungle river where they would strip off their clothes and bathe and Ken would practice fancy dives. In the late afternoon when they reached a village, their first visit would be to a jail where they would talk to the prisoners and give out Gospel tracts. They held street meetings where possible, or smaller Bible readings in the homes of Christians who invited them. Nights were spent wherever there was a bed—sometimes in the home of a rancher, several times with Chinese merchants, where they watched games of Chinese dice and ate exotic foods; frequently in the thatch-roofed homes of peasants where the food might include tortillas, *gallo pinto* (rice and beans fried with onion), *pinolillo* (a drink made of ground rice, peanuts, and chocolate), or plantains. There were many diversions during the evenings. Their duties of evangelization presumably discharged the two men joined in dancing to the music of a marimba, fished in the rivers, played a game called *Pajarito*, smoked marijuana (unwittingly, while staying with a man who trafficked in the weed—he did not reveal to them until later what he had given them), sang to the music of a guitar, and one night Hernán even rode a bull, but refused to allow Ken to try it because he felt responsible to Ken's mother for his safe return. Throughout the trip Ken was "very happy and joyful," his friend recalls, but when he returned to his work at the Institute the whole trip came before him in a different light. The journey itself, for the evangelization of an untouched district, he could report on with enthusiasm and the satisfaction of work done for the Lord. But his behavior during the trip he could not report on. Back in the atmosphere of the Institute, under the eye of his mother and other missionaries, he saw the dancing and smoking as wholly inconsistent with his aims as a missionary. It appeared to him again, as it had in seminary days, as sin, and he was overwhelmed with remorse. He went to Hernán and confessed with tears his reprehensible conduct, and went next to a missionary, calling himself a hopeless apostate. Finally he made a public apology in the Institute chapel.

Mr. and Mrs. Strachan made a journey to the United States during the following school year, and left the main responsibility of the work in their son's hands. He wrote to them regularly, reporting on the attendance in prayer meetings and Sunday church services, on the progress of the students and the spiritual state of some of the converts, on the missionaries themselves (one lady, he decided, must not be truly called of God since she was a poor teacher and in poor health), and on the condition of his own soul, ("I'm not getting anywhere in Bible study.") Meetings, however, which constituted the principal activity of his life, were described in these letters as "lovely," "very nice," "successful," "fine," or "worthwhile." There is evidence, however, that the young missionary was not always content with his role, and his mother's conviction that he needed a wife began to be his. After his parents returned to Costa Rica Ken made a trip to the States with the principal object of visiting a certain girl whom he had met in Dallas. She seemed to be the only one that presented herself to his mind as a prospect, and by this time he was lonely enough and restless enough to believe that steps must be taken. He went first to Columbia, South Carolina, to visit his sister Grace in college, and during that Christmas vacation was invited to a house party with her and several others, including "a certain young lady of your acquaintance. Go easy, Mother!" His mother had obviously mentioned Elizabeth Walker to Ken. He made it a point to talk with her, and by the end of the party had spent some long hours in her company.

From Columbia he went to Dallas and found his way to the door of the girl he wanted to see. Would she be glad to see him? What was an even more serious question, Would he be as glad as he had thought he would be to see *her?* Was she, after all, the kind of Christian he wanted for a wife? She was a Presbyterian, but was that enough? How deep did her religion go? He had thought and dreamed about her, but somehow his thoughts and dreams began to crumble as he approached her house in the taxi. He prayed all the way there, "Lord, show me definitely if this is Your will." The taxi stopped. He paid his fare, got out, and walked up to the door. This was it. He rang the doorbell. She appeared. "No," said his heart—or was it the Lord?—"No, it's finished." "I was free," he wrote later. They went out together and spent the evening conversing about the "things of the Lord." Ken learned that she had drifted away from such interest, and he said goodbye. "We'll probably never meet again, but if at any time I could help you. . . ." He felt like shouting all the way back to his hotel.

Well, if this wasn't the girl, it must be the other one. In February Ken went to see Elizabeth Walker in Wheaton. He summoned all his courage and took her out to dinner. "Mother, I have been praying that the Lord would lead me very definitely and I can't help but feel that He is, but as yet the way hasn't opened up clearly. When I get back, I want to have a long talk with you."

Possibly the way did not open up clearly because he himself did not open up clearly to Elizabeth regarding his feelings. He expected her, instead, to reveal herself, and explained many months later that he was put off by her casual manner, her "drawing-room conversation," and a "colorless pacifism." She should have known, he protested, that he was reaching for something, trying to break through her reserve, but the chances are good that the reserve was mainly his. On Valentine's Day he did manage to send her a bunch of red roses, but his courage failed him when it came to signing the card, and the best he could do was "Sincerely, Ken." Elizabeth had enough other interests to occupy her, and the bashful young missionary returned to his field with a "Reverend" before his name (he was ordained at Berachah Church in Philadelphia in February of 1939) but without the prize he had determined to win.

Shortly before arriving home he recieved word from his mother of his teaching assignment, and wrote, "I note in the assignments of teaching for next year that you have cut me out of my New Testament Synthesis class with the first-year students. *I protest*. Please don't take that away from me. I've been making plans for it ever since graduation and I don't want to give it up. You have assigned me less than last year and I take it as an insult. No kidding, Mother, at least give me NTS."

In March, 1939, the name of the mission was changed from the Latin America Evangelization Campaign to the Latin America Mission (LAM).

A few letters were exchanged between Ken and Elizabeth after he returned to his work, but hers were "cold and conventional" in Ken's opinion, and his "ambiguous" in hers. In the summer that followed the correspondence bogged down altogether.

Nearly a year went by, during which Ken's restlessness and discontent were not alleviated. He found it so difficult to work under his parents' jurisdiction, and the old doubts about his qualifications for the job tormented him so that he finally sought escape by attempting to join the Canadian Air Force. Patriotism, too, was a part of his motive, but his parents were not convinced that it was a wise move. Nevertheless they assisted him financially so that he was able to get as far as Panama where he thought he could enlist. He found to his dismay when he got there that he would have to pay his own passage all the way to Canada, and then he received a cable informing him that his mother had had a heart attack. Clearly there was nothing to do but go back home. His mother recovered, but relations were not improved, and when the senior Strachans were in the United States a short time afterward, Ken wrote a letter to his mother on her birthday. He wrote it out in longhand, corrected it, and copied it over carefully:

"Dear Mother, On Sunday you will be celebrating another birthday. It should be a happy one, in the new home with Gracie and possibly Father. I hope this letter will reach you in time, for in it I want to say something which I should have said long ago.

"I don't know just what has been responsible—whether the combination in me of Scotch reservedness with Irish explosiveness, or the fact that, having never truly had a home we have never learned to live together, or a restlessness on my part—maybe all of them— but I know that in the past three years since I came to work in Costa Rica I have fallen far short of what I should have been in relation to you and Father. . . .

"Mother, I do love you. I don't think you'll ever know how deeply I love you. I have always felt that in almost everything I was so very much like you, with the exception of your driving force. I don't know how to explain the coldness, thoughtlessness, and critical attitude on my part. If I have been reserved, almost cold at times, Mother, it has not been from lack of love. At times I have not felt free, as if I were here, not through a free choice or decision of my own, but because of the inevitableness of circumstances. I know that isn't true. Possibly it has been one of Satan's temptations that should have been resisted—but I know that many times it has checked spontaneous demonstrations of affection on my part.

"For the times of reserve I can only plead that it is my nature. Maybe if we were more together (could be without scrapping), confidences would come out more easily. For the many sins of omission and the acts of thoughtlessness I can only ask your forgiveness. I am ashamed that I can't carry on a conversation without getting heated and argumentative, losing my patience. My resolutions to do better have always been broken. I know that I am extremely selfish and self-centered and perhaps that is why I have been so critical and so unsympathetic and uninterested with your problems. In the three years that have passed I know I have hurt you many times. I'm sorry, Mother.

Kenneth with his mother, Susan B. Strachan

At Wheaton College, 1932

At Dallas. Ken wrote on the back of this picture, "Too cocky."

About 1926

About 1936

Elizabeth's engagement portrait, 1940.
Ken always had this one on his dresser.

December 27, 1940, Columbia,
South Carolina

In San José as new missionaries

With Harry, 1942

With Harry, Cathy, and Robert

"I don't want to say anything more. God helping me, I will do better from now on, and try to be to you what I could have and should have been in the past. I hope you have a happy birthday, and, God willing, Mother, I'll do my part to make this next year a happier one than the last. With love, your son, Kenneth."

She replied:

"My dear son, Your letter of 23rd got here on Saturday. I think the only thing I can say in reply is that it made me cry. I know you love me, Kenneth, therefore (but more because I love you) our little differences just fade away. I know that I have not been as helpful as I should at all times and am deeply sorry about it. Never mind, it will be better on before from every point of view."

CHAPTER 8

Kenneth Strachan had passed his thirtieth birthday when one of his mother's most importunate prayers was answered. In August, 1940, to his great surprise, he received an answer to a letter he had written to Elizabeth Walker in 1939. Although the correspondence had ground to a halt because Ken had never been able to bring himself to declare his true feelings, a friend had assured Elizabeth that it was a mistake to let the relationship die, that Ken still cared, and with this encouragement she wrote him a friendly letter. He sent her a stilted reply, suggesting that she "might care to exchange weekly letters," and this timid speculation was rewarded with an almost immediate jackpot of daily letters. Within days Ken had rehearsed the history of their ill-starred courtship, confessed his own cynicism and asked her forgiveness for having hurt her. "All my hopes and prayers prior to the Wheaton visit came to a dead end," he wrote, without realizing that he had not once told Elizabeth just what those hopes and prayers had been. Presuming that she was thoroughly aware of his feelings, he wrote freely about the meaning of *love*, following this with a paragraph on their own relationship which he carefully called *friendship*, and ending with a paragraph on his own understanding of the place of "the woman he loves" (not to say *wife*) in a man's life. Elizabeth took this to mean that he regarded her in this light and wondered if he were asking her to commit herself.

"No, I'm not asking that. But I couldn't love someone who is cold." Ken was not taking any chances of losing face by declaring his love until he could be quite sure he was loved. "I'm so shy that

52

unless a person meets me halfway I draw back into myself. I want a *warm* companionship." It was quite a lot for a man of his age to be asking of a girl that he had not seen for a year, and to whom he had dared to speak only in the most casual terms.

Ken made carbons of every one of his love letters, for mail flew back and forth between San José, Costa Rica, and Reidsville, North Carolina, with such breathtaking frequency that it was impossible to know otherwise which one Elizabeth was answering. No actual proposal or commitment had been made on either side when Ken revealed to her that he had, in his dark past, kissed a girl or two, but had never given his heart to anyone. "My heart is yours if you want it," was the nearest thing to a proposal that he could offer. Before he received her reply, he wrote, "I told you in my last that my heart was yours if you wanted it, and please, Elizabeth, say that you will take it. What I am trying to say is this—that I love you and want you and will you marry me? . . . If I were trying to tell you orally I would get choked up." He kept this letter on his desk for a day or so, reading and rereading it. Did he dare to mail it? At last he decided not to. It was too soon, too precipitous, to be so specific when he had as yet no assurance in black and white that she loved him. Surely that ought to come first? He lost nothing by this hesitation, for Elizabeth had read between the lines of the previous letter and wrote promptly that she was willing to marry him. "You are taking me quite by storm!" gasped Ken, but he was immensely relieved, and assured her that "life together may not always be easy but it will be interesting." A letter which crossed hers of acceptance said, "You will, won't you, dear? I'm taking it for granted." Then followed an involved and confusing exchange of letters concerning when and where the wedding should take place, Ken's original idea being that Elizabeth would come to Costa Rica. His mother helped him to see that it would be best for him to go to South Carolina. That question settled, it occurred to Ken to inquire about another— was it minor?—matter. How did Elizabeth feel about being a missionary? Had she ever felt called? Fortunately for him, she had.

But there was another thing, a possible barrier, which had better be seriously considered. Ken saw to it that his beloved cherished no illusions whatever about the kind of man she had just consented to marry. He was a villian, let there be no mistake about that. She had always lived on what he called a "high plane of spirituality"—he did not neglect to insert a parenthesis here, however, "(But was it real?)" —while he, on the other hand, existed on a "low plane of practical living which is one-sided and far short. . . . My life has been one of mostly downs and defeats, spiritual blindness and indifference, pride and selfishness." "I *am* sincere," he admitted, "but am probably just fooling myself when I say that as far as I know I have never tried to pretend to myself. There is very little honesty and moral strength in my character."

He described himself as having a "quick grasp, which makes me impatient with slow ones," as being "ambitious, but that's not necessarily bad if it's for the Lord's service," as having a "critical mind, but the Lord gave it to me and it has its use if rightly directed and controlled." He wrote of having to discipline two seminary students who had broken the rules. He called them in to his office separately, made them sit and wait while he pretended to be busy ("good old dean stuff") and then "I looked up and lit into them boiling mad." They were sufficiently terrified to satisfy him, and he told Elizabeth that after all, his bark was really worse than his bite.

"You'll find out in time that I am small about many things, a poor sport, unstable, impulsive, selfish, self-centered, shallow, and a spiritual failure," he warned her. "Don't judge by letters or appearances." At the same time, he made it clear that he must have a wife who would respect him. He could not bear, he told her, a "pitying mother-love."

There might be a few little redeeming features, however. "Am I a good packer? Yes! You wait and see! Yes, ma'am, I can change tires. Yes, ma'am, I can build fires (if I have enough matches). About fixing things around the house—maybe I'm a little weak."

Elizabeth, with the courage of love, accepted him, sure that his estimate of himself was grossly inaccurate. When he wrote, "Pray for me, that somehow I might get straightened out and not make a mess out of my life," she took this as a challenge, and gave herself to be his wife and his intercessor for the rest of his life.

It must be remembered that Ken Strachan had never before in his lifetime exposed himself so freely and so completely to another human being. He had never, except on the rarest of occasions, expressed his true feelings in words, either oral or written, and this sudden release of his soul, the terrible doubts that afflicted him at the slightest hint of reserve on Elizabeth's part, the maddening vagaries of the mail service between the two countries, the relatively slight acquaintance he had had with his fiancée before committing himself irrecoverably to her, and his soaring emotional ideals coupled with his intensely practical and pragmatic mind combined to make the four months of their "mail-order courtship," as he called it, both blissful and painful, hopeful and terrifying, revelatory of the man and at the same time misleading. The demands he made on his betrothed were wildly unrealistic, and her cheerful submission to them unbelievable. Perhaps, however, this is simply the story of romantic love wherever it occurs, and the success of the marriage that began so tempestuously is evidence that more was involved than mere passion.

"From your letters which arrived today I began to comprehend the truth of the old saying that the course of true love never runs smooth," Ken wrote on September 29, 1940. "I wish more than anything else that I could take you in my arms and comfort you and take away your blues and your doubts. . . . I love you so much that I can't find ways to tell you, and I think about you so constantly that my work suffers for it. Today, Sunday, I drove up to the farm. . . . There was a little service in place of Sunday School and I sat by an open window and looked out at the mountainside and dreamt of you, and thought of the strolls we would have over the farm when you come down, and I guess a smile must have been on my lips because all of a sudden I was aware that everybody was looking at me and laughing, and then I suddenly realized that the speaker had cracked some joke at me and caught me smiling like an idiot in the middle of a daydream."

Both man and woman possessed restless, inquiring minds, which compelled them to state and restate, define and redefine, and this led to difficulties in the interpretation of their love for one another. Elizabeth, a Southerner, wanted to be "adored." This word was scarcely included in the vocabulary of the missionary, and he replied, "I don't know just what you mean by the word 'adore.' If you mean worship, I guess it's true that I'll never worship you or anyone else. Perhaps I am overly critical, I don't know, but I am just as critical of myself as of anyone else, and knowing myself and all my faults and shams and petty egotism, I could never worship myself, and would find it very difficult to blind my eyes to the human characteristics of any person. To be frank I think I'll probably be quite aware of your faults, as you will of mine, so I suppose you'll never be able to get from your husband the one thing you've always wanted, adoration. And if you've wanted that just for the satisfaction of your vanity, it's just as well that you never get it. . . . I'll admire you but not for brilliance or physical beauty, I'll respect you but only for your integrity of character. I'll want to take you in my arms and whirl around on the floor in a jig at times, and at others I'll probably feel like crawling on the floor and kissing your feet. I want to have the quiet confidence that my honor, my being, my future, my life, are deposited in your keeping and know that whatever happens they'll be safe there and that you'll understand, and I want you to feel the same way about me, that in my heart above myself or anything else next to the Lord I'll have you. I'll want to take you out some nights to see the moon dreaming over the valley, and let the night whisper to you all the nameless, throbbing love for you that I could never express with my lips in the plain light of day. I want you to cry in my arms and I want to cry in yours. I want to be your husband, your lover, your pal, your partner, and I want you to be my wife, my sweetheart, my friend, my inspiration, and my counsellor. I can't describe my feelings, only I guess that after you added it all up you would still feel that it didn't sum up to adoration, and if in your estimate what I offered did not make up for it, I still could not say that I would adore you in the sense of 'worship.' "

Ken asked of Elizabeth an "unconditional love" which would not be affected in the slightest by any variation in his love. When she protested that she could not worship equally whether he were indifferent or responsive, he asked for a retraction of this reservation, or "we can't make a go of it." He did not hesitate to require of her what he was not willing himself to give. "If I have asked you to give yourself it has only been because I felt that I must be sure of your love for me and because only that way could I give myself entirely to you." There was much discussion back and forth on this point, Elizabeth trying to make Ken see that she was asking only what he asked of her. No, he answered, "I insist on sacrifical love on the part of the wife. You've got to give yourself to me the way I want you to."

Ken asked for a photo of Elizabeth, and promised to send her one of himself, but warned her that he now had a moustache. Had he *really?* "Yes, I have one and intend to keep it. I need it in order to look older and more dignified in my profession as a preacher and teacher, and especially as a single man." Well, said Elizabeth, I won't accept a picture of you wearing a moustache. "Are you sure you won't?" wrote Ken. She was sure. Off came the moustache, a picture was taken, and she was happy.

"You think I have a monogamous spirit," Ken wrote. "You mean you hope I have. I doubt whether there are many such men nowadays, so the only way that you can be sure of keeping me is by keeping my love." Lest she should misunderstand what he meant by this, he wrote in a later letter, "Libby, don't ever get possessive about me, or if you feel that way, don't show it too much. All I am and all I have is yours . . . but I will never allow myself to be tied to anyone's apron string. Don't look on me as a man God sent you in answer to your prayers. . . . It will be my greatest pleasure and privilege to serve you. I don't know why I said this except that when I looked at you in the snapshot I thought from the expression on your face you would be wanting to manage me later on. And Elizabeth, there's nothing I'd love better than being managed by you but don't forget that you must do it diplomatically."

Ken wrote out clearly his requirement of obedience: she "must" obey him, she "must" love him, she "must" take care of herself. But he surrendered to her charms at the same time, and said, "Libby, my darling, I think I'm going to like you, and already I'm afraid that I'm going to end up by adoring you madly and worshipping you, just when I said I would never do that, and it's going to be bad for you because it will go to your head and you will make me eat dust all my life." He promised over and over his unfailing consideration, generosity, thoughtfulness, and unselfishness, and with a disarming candor and failure to note the contradiction told her not to expect too much thoughtfulness from him because he was basically selfish. He turned over to her all money matters, making her from that point on secretary and treasurer, since he himself was "helpless as a child, with no head for figures." Elizabeth was delighted, and wrote that she would, in fact, rather do it than leave it to him. That was a bit much for Ken, and he was hurt by the implication that what he had said about himself might be accepted by Elizabeth as quite true.

Introducing themselves to one another proved to be a touchy business. He was "shocked" to learn that she was a Baptist. He was offended when she told him, in a casual way, that she had been president of her literary society in college. He took this as a subtle form of boasting and told her he was never impressed by human importance. He wanted her to know, of course, that he himself was "a British subject and proud of it," but told her flatly, "I have no use for snobbishness of any kind, whether of position, ability or intellect. I'd hate to think that you loved me because you thought that I had a certain amount of ability, that my prospects for the future were good, or any such rot as that. And don't ever expect me to love you because you are well-bred, or have a charming personality or have poise or a fine intellect, because I won't. What I'll love you for is because you're you, with all your little weaknesses and faults. And why I should love you already is something that I could never explain."

There were certainly some fine distinctions being drawn, and his letters must at times have been for Elizabeth what George Eliot calls a "severe mental scamper." It is not surprising that she chided him gently for being a bit Platonic. "Platonic?" he countered, "My letters Platonic? Here are three kisses for you X X X—the middle one is Platonic. Which did you like best?"

There is no escaping the recognition that Ken Strachan believed he had at last found what he wanted, and his love is poured out on page after page of thin paper. No matter what the hour, or how tired he might have been from his work, hardly a night passed when he did not sit down at his typewriter, carefully slip in a first sheet and a carbon, and tell Elizabeth that he loved her.

"I seem to have been transported all of a sudden and undeservedly from the dry barren wilderness in which in one very true sense my life had been cast, to Paradise, and all that in the space of a month."

He bought her a diamond ring which arrived in time for her to wear it to an announcement party given by her friends. With the ring went these words:

"Dearest: It would have been so much nicer if I could have been there to slip this ring on your finger and tell you at the same time something of what it means to me and what I mean by it.

"Sometimes when an object is used to represent some truth or relationship, its material quality and value eclipse its significance, and its spiritual value is forgotten. I hope you won't be thinking of this ring in terms of its material worth. It is unpretentious and simple and so is my love for you. In giving it to you I'm not doing it for the sake of custom or with the thought of its material worth, but because I want to express with it that which, had our courtship been a normal affair, I would have been able to express in many other ways in the course of time.

"And so, dear, with this ring I pledge my love, simply and unreservedly, now, not waiting until the marriage ceremony. With it I offer little in worldly goods or prospects, but all my heart and love for always. In its unbroken circle may it truly speak of the love which beareth all things, believeth all things, hopeth all things, endureth all things, never faileth. And may its tiny stone speak of the purity, sincerity, and transparency of that love.

"And dear, all I ask is that you recognize and cherish its preciousness and worth, for it carries all that a man can offer to the woman he loves. Ken.

"October 19, 1940."

Few bachelors can have anticipated marriage with higher hopes than Ken's—"the most sweet and sacred intimacy and communion in our oneness, but we shall look on our oneness as one solitary instrument in the Lord's service, and I think that we shall come nearer to plumbing the depths of human joy and happiness because of that."

"I want our life together to be the one great abiding fact of our existence."

"All my life I have loved teamwork."

"I like to think of you sewing, but more of you reading to me while my head is in your lap."

"Don't you think you would like to learn your Spanish verb conjugations in my arms? . . . Afternoon walks when the sun is setting. . . . What would *you* like to do? How do you know we'll get along? I'm half Latin, and it's difficult for different races to adjust. . . . Elizabeth, can you cook?"

He quoted Robert E. Speer as having said that Jesus' view of marriage contemplated it not as in indulgence but as a discipline, and Ken added that constant vigilance would be the price they must pay for success.

He promised Elizabeth that she need never fear that his work would take precedence over his home. His work, he said, had never been that important to him. There were countless occasions in the years that followed which, if Elizabeth had remembered the promise, would have caused her to wonder at its meaning.

As for children, "I guess I'd be satisfied with half a dozen or so provided they didn't make too much noise." The vague possibility of problems did enter his consciousness from time to time—children might, after all, make noise.

"Dear, do you suppose we'll ever have any quarrels?" he asked. Elizabeth was quick to assure him they would. In fact, she suggested, she might find herself having to forgive him ninety-nine times, and on the hundredth her love might turn to hatred. This prospect haunted Ken and he begged her to promise him that she would never hate him. When she admitted to having occasional moods and fits of depression he was ready with the solution to that little problem. "There's nothing to cure a fit of depression like a good beating. The world can't help but seem different after that."

Ken's extreme caution in expressing himself on paper is evidenced in the total absence of any mention of his own physical hunger. Only in the most delicate way did he skirt the subject in his letters, asking Elizabeth's advice as to some instructive reading they might both do, for, he confided, he was fairly ignorant and shy about such matters. When Elizabeth warned him that she had to sleep with her hair in bobby pins he was incredulous. "Do you mean that every other night you'll have your head full of steel points? How on earth do you expect to nestle up against me if your head is like a porcupine's?"

A few strict rules were drawn up in the course of their correspondence which were to govern their married life: No debts. No children for the first year ("I want you all to myself," Ken said). A solemn pact never to show displeasure with one another in public. No extravagances (Elizabeth was not to bring "too many worldly goods" with her to Costa Rica, "but if the Lord gives you silver it will be nice and we can enjoy it"); food was to be simple (among Ken's favorites: tea, cold milk, meat, and "Irish potatoes, first, last, and all the time"); candy was a major American vice, in Ken's opinion, and "childish besides"; Elizabeth must determine to master the Spanish language; they were both to be exemplary in conduct because they were the son and daughter-in-law of the mission founders; they would be strongly insistent of their independence and personal freedom from the senior Strachans, but generous in their gratitude to them; Elizabeth was not to be a drudge—there would be a "little servant girl" and Elizabeth would be regarded as a "lady with a lady's rights." The one big question which gave them both pause was that of Christian morality. Elizabeth was a firm believer in the keeping of the "law," and had been reared in an atmosphere of Puritanical separation from the "world" and a legalistic view of what it means to live the Christian life. She saw things in black and white. Ken had rebelled against this type of teaching when a student at Wheaton, where he scorned and repeatedly broke the pledge outlawing drinking, dancing, smoking, card playing, and any kind of theater. He was still torn by the conflicts these rules produced in his own mind, carrying on a continual argument with himself. Referring to Sunday "blue laws" which Elizabeth endorsed, Ken wrote, "No child of mine will have such rules imposed on him." He felt that Jesus and the apostle Paul set examples of liberty in personal behavior and that the Fundamentalist view of "separation"—though he had partially capitulated to it—was extreme and not defensible from Scripture. Elizabeth was troubled by what seemed to her a low standard of Christianity, and suggested that when Ken came up they should together consult a Bible teacher for whom she had a great respect, on "some of the weightier matters of the law." "That's one thing we won't do," replied Ken. "I prefer to do my own thinking. I may make a lot of mistakes and it may take me all my lifetime to evolve a connected and logical system of doctrine, but I'd rather do it that way. . . . I promise to accept all valid arguments but will not believe a thing because you or Dr. M——— believes it. I very definitely believe in tolerance, even of one's own immediate family."

Plans were finally laid for the wedding, which was to be more elaborate than Ken would have chosen. He had seen a "native" wedding in the lowlands of Costa Rica which appealed to him for its simplicity and he wrote to Elizabeth expressing his hope that theirs would be simple. He wanted to wear an ordinary suit "because we're missionaries and not justified in the extra expense" that a morning coat would have required. He made it clear, however, that Elizabeth was to do the choosing, and consulted her as to who his ushers should be. He also asked for suggestions about the honeymoon and about the amount of money he would need when he arrived. The arrival itself posed a question which each wrote about several times. Just what was to happen when Ken alighted from the train in Greenville? Would he kiss her? No, he expected her to fly up and throw her arms around him and kiss him, "because if you don't do this I will think that you don't trust me and I am a stranger." On second thought, he wondered if a public kiss was not perhaps unseemly for a missionary. Might they be too embarrassed, too shy, to kiss anyway? Neither was quite certain, and asked the other. No, said the other, there would be no reason to be embarrassed.

The days and weeks dragged by, the letters continued, gaining in assurance and warmth and eagerness. Ken saw that he had been an awkward suitor, and confessed that he had been "too quixotic and exacting, braying like an ass, demanding of you what I should have given myself." He gave up asking for an unconditional surrender or implicit obedience, and told Elizabeth that they would be just "partners in everything." He saw their lives as two streams, merging, or as two parts of a whole, which God had fashioned and forged in different parts of the world and then, in a "wonderful revelation of His love and plan for each" had brought together. Elizabeth was, Ken declared, precisely what he wanted. "I used to want a strong, husky, athletic type, but no longer. I want someone feminine and womanly, and it's you. I'm no tall, broad-shouldered Romeo" (remembering, no doubt, that she had chosen him who was five feet six inches tall over several suitors who were tall, broad-shouldered Romeos), but Elizabeth's falling in love with him had established his faith in fairy-story endings in life.

She warned him that he must be careful always to give the impression that he had worked very hard to get her, although she knew that she had done 90 per cent of the courting. This he stoutly denied, which she admitted was what she had hoped he would do.

"Sweetheart," he wrote, "it's time for our date tonight and let's go strolling along the Milky Way and let's window-shop in all the stars of heaven, and let's thank God for the greatest gift of all, His love, and ask Him to keep us and bring us together in it. Libby dear, I love you and I'm coming to you. Wait for me, dearest.

Your sweetheart, Ken."

At last he was on the boat, and in a few days she received a telegram: ARRIVING GREENVILLE TUESDAY AS AGREED IMPATIENT LOVE YOU KEN.

There was a round of dinners, teas, and parties that for ordinary people would have been exhausting and hectic, but that Ken described in his letters to his mother as "wonderful," "grand," and "happy"—the first time such words had appeared in his letters referring to social activities. The wedding ceremony was performed on December 27, 1940, by Dr. Robert McQuilkin, president of Columbia Bible College, in the lobby of the college, followed by a reception in the dining hall. Mother Strachan wrote, "All day yesterday and especially at eleven A.M. I was with you in thought and prayer. . . . You know how wonderfully He plants seeds that bring fruitage in far distant times—'to the third and fourth generation of them that fear Me'—so may He do it for you."

CHAPTER 9

A large delegation of missionaries was at the station to welcome the newlyweds when they arrived in San José. Ken was proud and shy to introduce Elizabeth. She was baffled to discover that these whose lives were given to so serious a purpose found time for so frivolous an occasion as meeting a new bride and groom. Mother Strachan gave a gala supper in honor of the couple which, had Elizabeth known more than she then knew of the price and the difficulty of obtaining items like chicken, celery, and olives, would have baffled her even more.

Their first home was in the Institute, which had now become a seminary. It was an apartment consisting of two high-ceilinged rooms with no kitchen. They ate every meal in the common dining room with the students and other missionaries.

Ken showed Elizabeth around his beloved city with its lavish gardens of bougainevillea, hibiscus, belladonna, and royal palm trees; its parks and fountains, its narrow streets jammed with carts, small cars and wagons, bicycles and buses, its ragged peasants and elegant señoritas, its houses of painted wood or tinted adobe, its beautiful sunshine in the mornings and its rain in the afternoons.

Elizabeth, determined to be as good a missionary as a wife, exceeded all Ken's expectations in her efforts to learn Spanish, studying on her own eight hours a day. She fell short of them, however, in the results, and he found it difficult to understand why the language did not come to her with greater ease. For the first few months he was patient and hopeful, but at last began to wonder if his hopes were in vain. When she took up formal lessons years later, with no greater success, he said it was money down the drain. After having studied for only three months she was asked to make an announcement at the church in Spanish, and for this crisis she studied and worked, writing out word for word what she meant to say. When she rehearsed it for Ken she made mistakes. His humiliation was as great as hers, and he could not find it in him to commend her for the effort and courage which it had taken, since he himself had never known what it was to struggle with a completely unknown foreign language.

He was anxious that their conduct as son and daughter-in-law of the directors should be above reproach, and left no doubt in his wife's mind as to what was expected of her with regard to public meetings. She was to attend prayer meetings at six-thirty in the morning, go to church regularly on Sundays, and assist in some classes for children that a neighboring mission sponsored. For a man who had regarded church attendance for himself as above and beyond the call of duty his requirements during the early years of his marriage seem a trifle exacting, but he had found the woman who fulfilled his highest ideals and who—whether he would have admitted to reciprocal emotion in exactly the same terms or not— "adored" him, and he was charged with the determination to start out on the right foot, for once to do things as they ought to be done. He wrote out a list of rules to be observed in their home:

"1) Less turkey for missionaries and more chicken for the natives.

"2) No special privileges. Strict attendance at chapel, prayer meeting, once a week in Templo, and Sunday night services.

"3) No criticism.

"4) Family devotions.

"5) Honest measure of work.

"6) Neat dress, especially at evening meal. No personal subjects at table.

"7) Self-discipline in study and culture for future.

"8) Definite witnessing."

They had been married only five months when Ken made the first of hundreds of missionary journeys away from home. This time it was for a conference of missionaries in Guatemala, and each journey which followed was for purposes in keeping with his missionary calling. For the first few years it appears that Ken did not question the necessity of such travel, although as years passed and the percentage of time spent at home did not increase he had occasion again and again to wonder if there might not be another way of doing things.

The Strachans' first child was born in November, 1941, and although Elizabeth wished to name him after his father, Ken had long since made up his mind that his firstborn would be Harry Wallace, after his own father and brother. When Harry was a few months old the family moved to a place in the lower hills west of San José called Atenas for a few months of evangelistic work and more primitive living conditions than the seminary had provided. The house was discovered to have been built on top of an anthill; the stove was a sand table; lighting was a single bulb that came on at six o'clock every evening for a few hours; the only table in the house had to be used for eating as well as for Ken's study; the diet was limited mostly to oatmeal, rice, beans, and oranges. It was during this time that Ken read the two-volumn account of the life of Hudson Taylor of the China Inland Mission and as a result felt that he must increase the amount of money he gave to the Lord.

August of that year (1942) found Ken, Elizabeth, and little Harry in the United States, Ken studying at Princeton Seminary, Elizabeth juggling and stretching their tiny allowance first to provide for the three of them, and in February to cover the needs of four, when a daughter, Cathy, was born. When Ken had written his thesis on the Failure of the Reformation in Spain, and had received his degree of Master of Theology, he made a "deputation" tour in the Northeast during the summer.

It was ironic that while doing deputation—seeking to gain new prayer and financial support for the mission—Ken should have found himself sorely tempted by material things which he had renounced, and tried also in the matter of the certainty of his personal call to missionary service. While visiting a resort in Pennsylvania he wrote to Elizabeth describing the elegant dinner he had been served, telling her how badly he missed having her with him, and adding, "The beauty of a place like this is bad on one's morale. I can sense it. Makes you start dreaming of owning such a place and taking one's ease in it and forgetting the heat and sweat and tears of the valley where God's work is to be done. At times I wonder how firm my convictions are with regard to our calling to Latin America. How would you like for me to have a job teaching in some seminary and spending our summers at our own cottage at some lovely mountain lake? 'Get thee behind me!' "

Another letter from the same resort repeats the above thoughts, followed by "I began to wish that the Lord would open up a nice comfortable teaching job for us up here in the States. And from that my thoughts went to Costa Rica and the problems there and the prospects. Somehow the outlook didn't appeal to me any too much, but then the Lord brought to mind the fact that the very things which I wanted up here in the States were so very illusory and uncertain—and that He would recompense somehow or other."

He and his wife had been thinking about the future leadership of the LAM, and it was natural that Ken would wonder if he was ultimately to fit into that place. A conflict arose in his mind at the thought—he wanted the position, yet he did not want the burdens it entailed. He wanted to serve the Lord "full time" yet he found other prospects appealing. While away on this speaking trip he wrote to Elizabeth: "The feeling came to me that instead of going down and trying to push ourselves forward we should leave the matter with the Lord, and wait patiently for Him to act and decide. Anyway, look how much He has blessed us and the happiness He has brought us, and we must trust Him for the unknown future as it concerns us and the children." And later, "On thinking over our situation in the mission I feel at times that perhaps it would be good for me to resign, and yet I feel definitely it is the Lord's place for us. If there were only some way of getting across to some of the others (without appearing to be thinking about it) that we did not have any personal ambitions as far as the mission is concerned (or have we??). If you had to choose between my making quite a success in Christian circles but not being able to live at home very much, or making no professional progress but having an ideal home life, which would you choose? I don't think I'd have much trouble deciding."

This was their longest separation in the two and a half years of their marriage, and it was tiresome for Ken, who wrote every day during the summer loving, lonely letters to Elizabeth, of which the following is a sample:

"Letter to 'one and only'—

"Dear Sweetheart:

"Scene: Third floor of a three-story house. Hot! Late at night! Tired! Lonely! Homesick!!! Hero has been in New York—a successful day on the whole but hard on his dogs and his laundry bill. . . . Hero definitely needs a mate. Might as well be marooned on an island.

"Plot: Hero spends some thought upon qualifications he would like to see in mate-to-be (if he ever gets married again). First, heroine must be beautiful and shapely with a patrician air. Secondly, she must have that intangible something that commands respect and yet stirs the blood at the same time. Thirdly, she must be to him (the hero) in life a playmate . . . consoling, restoring, encouraging. She must be his lover and between them they must tend the flame of love and youth and life. She must be his wife, mother, sister, little girl all in one. Fourthly, she must ever be at his side. (This is most important!)

"Unfolding of Plot: (Plot does not thicken) Hero suddenly discovers that qualifications he has listed as requisites were merely a few things that could be ennumerated in describing a 'beautiful young bride who refused to sleep' (on a certain occasion).

"Grand Finale: To be continued.

"Dearest, I'm so dead tired I don't know what I'm writing, and am only conscious of a deep unhappy longing. I want you."

When they returned to Costa Rica in August Ken took up his work again at the seminary, but with a new enthusiasm and some new ideas formulated at Princeton. It was clear to him that the mission could not function as a service organization to other missions without the cooperation of those missions. Where there were misunderstandings and jealousies he wanted to make amends, and within a month or two was off on a trip with that object in view, visiting other countries in Central America where there were Bible institutes, and missions whose good will he sought. He was inexperienced, he was aware of his own weakness and he made an honest effort to overcome his handicaps. "Tried my best not to get intense and did not try to refute directly any criticism or objection that was raised," he wrote to his wife. Again the traveling seemed a necessary evil. "Don't go much for this traveling around. Don't see how Father kept it up for so long.

. . . Sometimes I feel so keen and enthused about the work, at other times indifferent and tempted to wish my life were cast in secular spheres."

January and February of 1944 were spent in travel, this time with a view to helping small rural churches to organize. While at Princeton the importance of the local, visible church had been brought to Ken's attention, and he saw that it was an area hitherto neglected by the LAM which had been established only for evangelistic work. He found small bodies of believers in the backwoods of Guanacaste struggling along without system or order. Of a visit to one of these congregations he wrote:

"The last lap of the ride here was taken through gigantic forests— tall timbers swaying over a hundred feet above us, and trails still wet and muddy from last winter's rains—frequent crossing of icy-cold mountain streams. It was beautiful, and finally we came out on tiny clearings on the northwest slope of the hills facing Volcán Tenorio. This isn't Guanacaste, it's the frontiers, where isolated homesteads are waging a constant fight against the wilderness, the wind and rain. And here there is a precious group of believers headed by Don Pedro Espinosa.

"He welcomed us with wild pleasure, shouting in a shrill, barking voice. He is constantly bubbling over with enthusiasm (of fifteen years' duration) and loves the Lord like a little child. When he speaks the words come out in a torrent, disjointed, explosive, sometimes high and shrill, then suddenly lowered, and difficult to follow, but through his speech you can't help realizing that he knows the Lord, and more, the Lord knows him and has revealed Himself to him. You should hear him pray—he screams the words out, each sentence unrelated to the previous—drops his voice and pleads for the Lord's blessing on those present, interrupts himself to bark out 'and forgive me a poor sinner'— and then goes on. And you should hear him sing hymns with a guitar. He moans, sways over the guitar, croons, suddenly yells out triumphantly, twists and warps a hymn so you hardly recognize it, but out of the almost crazy jumble he makes you feel all the agony and pain of the crucifixion and all the joy and triumph of the Christian life. I've never seen anyone quite like him.

"Yesterday afternoon we had a meeting from four to six and then another last night. Today from nine to eleven, and from three on—and so on, every day through Sunday. (On Sunday five services including a baptismal service) Wish I could tell you how much all this transforms and sharpens one's concepts of church and religious services."

A letter written in El Dos de Cañas tells of another "church":

"I've thought of you most of the day as we climbed steadily up the mountains. I don't think I've ever climbed as much on horseback as this morning. We climbed past several gold mines and kept on rising until we could see the whole gulf with all its islands, and off in the distance the peninsula of Puntarenas and the penal island of San Lucas. . . .

"Yesterday we had quite a time of it. We set off on foot under the noon sun for the half hour walk to the hut of the brother where we were to have a brief preaching service before proceeding to the river for the baptism service. It was about as hot in the little hut as it had been on the road. While we waited for all the brethren to congregate (just to show you how funny we human beings are) the man of the house said, 'I suppose in the course of your trips you visit many a poor hovel without any comforts such as we enjoy.' I looked around his place, the low tin roof, mud floor, bed of boards partly hidden from the rest of the room by some rough hewn boards, primitive fireplace, old nail barrel which held the water brought up from the river two hundred yards away—glanced past him through the wide cracks of the walls to the barren little patio baking in the sun outside, and solemnly agreed with him.

"It would have thrilled you to see the utter simplicity of the whole prolonged service that afternoon. We wound down the path to the river, picked out a pool, put on our white robes, and held the baptisms. It was primitive, but I couldn't help feeling that baptismal fonts inside of churches were a poor affair in comparison. I felt sorry for us who have missed the thrill of the blessing those folks received yesterday afternoon. After that, back to the house—coffee and *rosquetes*—then a business session in which the church was organized and elected its officials, and then the Lord's supper, preceded by testimonies."

Not long after Ken returned home from the lowlands he was in the hospital with an intestinal infection. In another room was his small daughter Cathy, also ill. In a third lay Elizabeth, who had just given birth to a son, Robert Kenneth, Jr.

Ken was soon out of the hospital and off again, this time to Guatemala, and later back to the lowlands of Guanacaste. He felt certain of the value of these visits, with their objective of self-governing, self-propogating, organized churches. He wrote of the "quiet satisfaction of carrying Gospel tracts to little huts tucked away in the mountainsides," but he could not escape the feeling now and then that what he really wanted was to resign from the mission and settle down on a farm. At other times the idea of staying with the mission and making his contribution by thinking and writing rather than by preaching and traveling appealed strongly to him.

The last night of 1944 found Ken in Columbia at the annual meetings of the LAM. He suggested to Elizabeth that they make Hosea 6:3 their verse for the coming year: "Let us know, let us press on to know the Lord; His going forth is sure as the dawn, he will come to us as the showers, as the spring rains that water the earth."

"After the meeting," he wrote, "I got a rocking chair and went out under a tree in the yard and had a little time of prayer by myself thinking of the New Year. . . . I was glad that I could sort of commend you and myself and each of the children to the Lord for the whole of the coming year. And dearest, I prayed that the Lord would meet all the need and desire of your heart and lead us both out into a greater ministry for Him. As we've travelled around it has made me more conscious of the vastness of the world and the need and the great possibilities of service for the ones who allow themselves to be used of God."

CHAPTER 10

In April, 1945, Harry Strachan, Ken's father, died. It was he who had, in addition to founding the mission, traveled more extensively than any other Protestant missionary for the cause of evangelization in Latin America. He had also taken the full responsibility for scouting recruits, and raising financial support for the mission. When he died, the mantle fell on his son Kenneth, who left Costa Rica almost immediately for another deputation trip to Mexico and the United States. He found himself "pushed into the harsh cold world and things will never be the same. Responsibility—I don't like it!" Besides interviewing prospective missionaries and donors, Ken began to consider the possibilities of radio and literature work for the mission, and spent much time and energy seeking out those who might help in these fields. He was excited by the personal contacts which this work entailed, but depressed by the public appearances he was forced to make, and wrote to Elizabeth:

"Here I am in big-time competition where one has to be shrewd as a horse trader and know how to boost himself and how to work people in order to get ahead. It's all in the Christian world, and yet there seems to exist a sort of code among Christian leaders, etc., such as might exist in wordly competition. It would appear that modern publicity and promotion are necessary to raise money for any Christian enterprise, but that doesn't mean that one doesn't look to the Lord but merely that one uses the best up-to-date methods for presenting the need so that the Lord may touch people's hearts to give, and yet I can't help wondering whether we should not look

more to the Lord and avoid modern publicity. . . . I instinctively
dislike promotional publicity."

It was here, when Ken was for the first time *responsible*, that he
began to examine the actual working of the evangelical mission
scene. What he saw now and then disturbed him—could it be that
there were inconsistencies, contradictions, even phoniness? Or was
there something twisted about his own view? Others seemed to accept with ease what he found uncomfortable, so perhaps he was
wrong, would see it differently later on. The questions raised were
often put into letters to his wife, but seldom articulated elsewhere.
Usually, as in this case, he tried to give himself answers: "One has
to be shrewd. . . . It's all in the Christian world and yet. . . . It would
appear . . . but that doesn't mean. . . . Yet I can't help wondering.
. . . I instinctively dislike. . . ."

Other letters from this tour reflect Ken's sustained hope that the
need for travel would not last much longer (this, in spite of the
obvious lack of anyone else to take his father's place); his repeated
insistence that he was not in a position to speak positively to others
about victorious Christian living; and his gloomy, almost desperate
fits of homesickness for his wife and children.

As the representative of a nondenominational "faith" mission he
found it difficult to steer a clear course between the Fundamentalists
and the Inclusivists, whose controversies were highly distasteful to
a man of such vision for cooperation. "It is hard," he wrote, "not to
be drawn into the controversy. So much of the Come-Outers' attention is fixed on the sins of the Inclusivist churches—it comes out in
their prayers, sermons, remarks. I don't feel at home, and it makes
me want to go into regular denominational missionary work." Probably the tensions which existed between these groups and their suspicion of anyone who refused to stand firmly on one side or the
other account in part for Strachan's failure to gain much support
during the trip. He took the blame himself for the scanty receipts,
attributing them to his being a "flop, unable to speak openly about
money," and as yet unconvinced of the methods used by "faith"
missions. Without conviction, however, he pursued his dogged
course, reminding himself and Elizabeth that the misgivings must be
his own lack of faith if the Lord had called them here. He accepted

as well as he could the prevalent belief among evangelicals that the methods employed in the Lord's work had been devised by spiritually minded men under the guidance of God, and hence must be His.

There was another area in which Ken was waging a still unresolved battle. It was the question of Christian conduct. He could not wholeheartedly endorse Elizabeth's firm belief that a Christian must adhere to certain fixed laws regarding the keeping of the Lord's Day, the kind of amusements allowed, indulgences such as smoking and drinking, and certain modes of dress. To Ken, such things were conditioned by time and place, and not to be determined by any immutable laws. Principles were for him of far more consequence than visible, tangible things. When he married Elizabeth he had chosen to please her in every possible way, and submitted to her "rules" without believing that these were necessarily required by God. It simplified things for him in the mission as well as at home, since most of their constituency shared Elizabeth's views. But the matter would not rest there, and from time to time raised its head for his fresh consideration. One of these times was while he was traveling in Illinois in May, 1945.

"Dearest, for the last week or so I've been struggling all over again with the problems of Christian liberty and separation (and you know how our views differ). Last night it dawned on me that while Paul's principles (not laws) as applied to different consciences, environments and backgrounds, would determine different norms of behavior for different individuals, yet that generally each individual's heredity, background, and environment is more or less a fixed thing for life, so that he may, guided by the Holy Spirit in the light of Scripture, discover what the Lord's will for him is as regards his conduct and relationships, and that norm will generally hold good for his lifetime. I don't know if I make myself clear, but it seems to me that this allows for the fluidity (which I have always insisted on) and yet avoids the vacillating tendency (which has always resulted from my position) and provides for the permanence and absolute stand which you have always insisted upon. It is still too early to say whether or not this is going to help me. I mentioned it, because suddenly while thinking of you, it came to me that loving you like I do as far as I was concerned I would accept your standards whether convinced or not simply because the greatest thing for me (humanly speaking) is you. In a way which I did not feel before (due perhaps to my argumentative nature) I feel that even though it meant not taking a dip on Sunday again in my life, I'd rather be and live at one with you. Do you understand what I mean, dear?"

There was always for Kenneth a degree of peace of mind achieved by articulating his questions and then giving them on paper what looked—to him, for a time, and to most of his associates—like answers.

Ken was invited to speak at Wheaton College. It was impossible for him to stand behind the chapel pulpit without remembering the years when he had sat in the pews and "was ruffled the wrong way having to listen day after day to small, unknown men who cannot talk well try to convert you to their field. Students shut their ears and often their eyes," as he had written in 1929. What was the point of it all? Something of the ambiguity of his feelings regarding the whole missionary-on-furlough role was expressed in *The Daily Reporter,* a little newssheet which he created to send to Elizabeth in place of the usual daily letter. It carries a headline, "Noted Missionary in College Chapel," and a sketch of a gesticulating speaker before a sea of faces. "May 29. With an excitement scarcely ever equalled in the history of the college, Wheaton's student body hung on the breathtaking words of one of Latin America's great missionaries. With hair graying from the stress of his years on the field, a body wracked with pain and stooped from the rigors of his pioneer work, Dr. R. K. Strachan told his audience a thrilling story. Students were profoundly moved, sobs were audible throughout the tense multitude, and some fainted, as he related the miraculous way in which little Chepita, one of Costa Rica's 130 million children was persuaded to go to Sunday School and learned to sing a chorus. Only the bell kept the emotions of the students from mounting to such a pitch that something unexpected might have been expected. Needless to say it was with much regret that both faculty and student body bade sad farewell to their illustrious visitor."

On page 3 of the *Reporter* the following "Drama" appears:

Title: THE DEPUTATION SPEAKER

Scene: Takes place in a telephone booth in a big city railroad station. Missionary has just got off the train and his suitcases are piled up outside the booth.

ACT ONE

MISSIONARY (muses out loud): Where am I going to sleep tonight? Should I get a hotel room first or would it be best to call Mrs. Bigbosom first? Perhaps she might invite me to stay at her home? (Missionary fiddles around, looks up Mrs. Bigbosom's number. Counts change in his pocket. Hesitates a while. Mops perspiration off his brow—it's hot in the phone booth. Finally decides to call up Mrs. Bigbosom.)

ACT TWO

Scene: Same telephone booth.

(Missionary dials on phone. No answer. Waits a long time while phone rings, meanwhile drawing figures with his finger. Still no answer. Hangs up. Goes outside booth to cool off.)

ACT THREE

Scene: Railroad station restaurant.

A lone figure is sitting on a stool reading a newspaper, with a doughnut in one hand and a cup of coffee on the counter before. Piled beside him against the counter are two heavy suitcases. It is a missionary. He looks lonely and unhappy.

ACT FOUR

Scene: Phone booth. Man inside. Two big suitcases outside.

MISSIONARY: Hello? Is this Mrs. Bigbosom?

MRS. B. Yes, this is Mrs. Bigbosom.

MISSIONARY: How do you do, Mrs. Bigbosom. This is David Livingstone from Costa Rica.

MRS. B. Whooo?

MISSIONARY: David Livingstone from Costa Rica.

MRS. B. Ohhh yeesss. Why Mr. Livingstone, it's so good to hear your voice. And how are you?

MISSIONARY: Just fine, thank you. I'm so glad . . .

MRS. B. And how are your dear parents? I remember them so well. Yes, yes, and you are now in the United States?

MISSIONARY: Yes, I . . .

MRS. B. Oh, I think you are doing such a wonderful work. I've been interested in the Latin America Evangelistic Crusade from the very beginning. Are you staying in the city very long?

MISSIONARY: Well, I . . .

Mrs. B. You know, Mr. Levinston, Fluffy—that's my little dog—has been under the weather recently. He has a bad cold. It has meant such an added burden for me, you know.

Missionary: That's too bad. I'm so sorry. I . . .

Mrs. B. And, Mr. Levinton, I would love so much to have you stay at our home or drop in for a visit, but with Fluffy sick it's absolutely out of the question. You might catch Fluffy's cold. It would never do. And besides I am almost distracted with it all.

Missionary: I understand perfectly, Mrs. Bigbosom. I . . .

Mrs. B. Yes, I am so sorry. You are doing such a marvelous work. When do you expect to return to the States? You must be sure to drop around the next time you come this way. I have been deeply interested in the work of your mission, yes, from the very beginning.

Missionary: Thank you, Mrs. Bigbosom. I . . .

Mrs. B. Yes, I'm sure. Well, thank you for calling. Now don't forget I *must* see you next time. Goodbye. . . .

ACT FIVE

Scene: Lobby of hotel. Figure of a man standing at registry window. Beside him are two heavy suitcases. He looks tired.

END OF DRAMA

In June the Home Council of the mission passed a resolution recommending that Kenneth Strachan be appointed co-director of the mission with his mother. He believed that a change must be made in his status as "deputy director" lest it leave doubt in the minds of mission supporters regarding his qualifications of eventual leadership. "This is not good for the mission and the public's confidence in the mission to have the matter in such an unsettled condition at this time." However, he was not to be railroaded into an acceptance of the new position without a clear understanding of his footing. "I will *not* accept the position upon the basis of my relationship to the folks, I would only accept the co-directorship at present on the condition that the matter was presented to the whole missionary family and that it was the unanimous will of the missionary family and the different councils," he told Elizabeth. He insisted also on a clear definition of the respective authority of the two directors so that there would be no overlapping or countermanding of orders; no individual action on the part of one without the other's approval; strict adherence to the terms of the new constitution; and complete co-control of all branches of the work such as the hospital, the seminary, and the church. So far as Strachan could see there was no contradiction implicit in the ideas of "no overlapping" and "complete co-control."

Hints of the deep respect which Ken felt for his mother are preserved in cards which accompanied a bouquet of red roses and a birthday gift. When his mother had an accident, Ken instructed Elizabeth to take some money from his book fund and buy her a "gorgeous bouquet of red, red roses." On the card she was to write, "Keep your Irish chin up. With ever so much love, Kenneth." With the gift he sent a note saying, "This is to express very inadequately my own personal admiration and love for you—not because of the years of service or the achievements thereof alone, but because of something that has to do with your own spiritual life and courage in times of testing, and because of a special relationship to you. Psalm 116:16 ['O Lord, I am thy servant, the son of thy handmaid. Thou hast loosed my bonds'] has meaning for me and I thank you and love you for it. Kenneth."

That a woman of such "aggressive gifts for taking charge and running things," as Kenneth put it, and a young man who was in the first place her son and in the second a man of inflammable temper and somewhat revolutionary ideas could have succeeded at all as co-directors of an organization is evidence of the reality of their mutual love and respect. When Ken returned to Costa Rica in July, "sick to death of being a visitor, speaking, travelling—no more deputation trips for me! Longing for home" and feeling that he had "aged a lot on this trip"—he accepted his new position with a will to make it work. He wanted his mother's last years to be years of peaceful happiness.

Among the first changes which Ken undertook to make were the appointing of a home director, and the formation of an association of churches in Costa Rica. Rodolfo Cruz, the Institute graduate from Guatemala, accompanied Ken during the summer of 1945 on a visit to the churches of rural areas. There were difficulties—Ken was irritated when he arrived at Río Chiquito to discover that the "one meeting a day" which they had asked him to conduct meant one meeting, from five in the morning until eleven at night. He and

Rodolfo had differences of opinion during the sessions for organizing churches, and Ken was capable of hot demonstration of his Irish temper. Rodolfo remembered him in later years always as a "faithful friend," and their public quarrels were publicly smoothed out. The result of this itineration was the formation of the Asociación de Iglesias Bíblicas, a step toward cooperation which afterward would pave the way for a far broader effort.

The Strachan family went to the United States in December for a year of furlough, and it was then that Ken bought his first car, a sport roadster for which he paid five hundred dollars. He was soon away in it, speaking and visiting in many states while Elizabeth, pregnant for the fourth time, stayed with the children in a "missionary apartment" in New Jersey. This apartment, provided gratis for missionaries on furlough, was a godsend, but there were aspects which seemed calculated to try the sanctification of the most devoted servant of the Lord. The washing machine Elizabeth described as "impossible," an adjective which her husband probably took with a grain of salt. He had little understanding of her situation as he traveled in his new Ford—at times the monthly allowance was simply not enough for necessities, and Elizabeth was so limited in time and strength that she occasionally found it necessary to send five-year-old Harry to the store for groceries—but Ken wrote, "You are the 'hero' in our family, and I know it, dear. When I think of all your love and patience and cheerfulness, my heart wells up with love for you and I feel there isn't anything too good for you."

They were back in Costa Rica by Christmas, and in January a second daughter, Clare, was born, and Ken left home for Colombia. "Give Daddy a safe trip and help him to bring us Chiclets when he comes back," the children prayed.

As a teacher in the seminary Ken had gained great popularity, not only because of his careful scholarship and interesting lectures, but because of his increasing ability to do what he had always said was one of the most difficult things for him to do: to take a personal interest in people. He knew not only the name of each student but the names of wife and children as well. This quality, though usually taken for granted in persons of lesser station, is impressive in a superior, and while Ken was conscious of the dignity and responsibility of his position he gave himself to the Latin people in a way which he would not do with fellow missionaries. To the latter, he was sometimes withdrawn and irritatingly independent, although always loyal. To the Latin he would give himself generously and sacrificially, and this quality won the respect of seminary students as well as others. Once there was a rebellion among the students which caused an administrative crisis in the institution. Other professors had attempted without success to mediate, and Ken called a meeting of the students in which he quietly stated that there must be a final seat of authority. If that authority lay with the students, clearly there could be no graduation or diplomas since an institution without authority to discipline was likewise without authority to issue degrees. The student leaders decided at that point that the rebellion had gone far enough. Ken assigned a faculty member as counselor to each student after this and relations were significantly improved.

Strachan's official status in the mission and his success in student relations did nothing to convince him in his heart of hearts that he was what he longed to be. The doing of spiritual work requires spiritual power. Ken was engaged in evangelization—the winning of souls, the bringing of men out of spiritual darkness and death into eternal light and life—and this, he believed, was simply an impossibility without the power of the Holy Spirit of God. "He that abideth in me, and I in him," Jesus had said, "the same bringeth forth much fruit: for without me ye can do nothing." *Nothing.* This knowledge tortured Ken.

"At times I feel that if I don't attain to a certain spiritual climax or summit I should retire entirely from active service," he wrote not long after his father's death. Without the one indispensable qualification, why go on? How could he go on? Had he a right to expect that God would supply what he lacked? He believed that he had, and he prayed.

The following year while he was in the southern states something happened. There is no written record of exactly what it was, but he believed at the time that God had at last broken through to him, had anointed him in a special way in Greensboro, North Carolina, so that he telephoned a close friend to share the joyful news that he had now been baptized with the Holy Spirit.

Ken's travels in 1948 included Colombia, Puerto Rico, Dominican Republic, Panama, Florida, Illinois, California, and New Jersey, where he made application for naturalization papers, having decided that it would be wise for the entire family to claim one nationality. He hunted recruits, visited seminary graduates, "gained a clearer perspective of steps to be taken to make our work known," and wrote loving and forlorn letters home. "Elizabeth sweetheart, when the wanderer far from home would fain turn his steps towards the blessed warmth but dare not because of duty's call, he is a sad lad, methinks. Poor wretch, that I am, my pilgrimage is far from over and I must tread this lonesome way for yet another moon or more. . . .

> Your ~~dutiful, sincere, patient~~
> adoring (that's the word!)
> admirer,
> Ken."

He did make it home in time to welcome into the world a third son, their fifth child, named John.

It would be comforting to find that his Greensboro experience was the answer to his need, but during the Inter-Field Council meetings in Colombia in the beginning of 1949 he wrote, "Dearest, the gears have been grinding and it's been hard pulling. It's not alone missing you, although I suppose that subconsciously it's one of the main factors—mostly it's a hard, selfish coldness and the doubt and fear about the forthcoming meetings. I'm not ready in any way and I don't see how God can bless and I'm sick of myself. . . . I know I'm too subject to feelings, but you can't imagine (maybe you can) how much spiritual and mental energy are burnt up in trying to fight things out. After going through days of this I can't help but long that somehow or other someday the Lord will bring me into a more or less permanent state of 'peace and joy in believing.' Not that I expect any 'experience' to deliver me from the blood, sweat, and tears of life or work. . . . One thing I know—that God gave you to me to help out with the job, perhaps because He knew it was going to be a tough one."

He spoke in the meetings referred to on "La Disciplina Cristiana," and one young Colombian woman remembers his manner of speaking as "so tender, so sweet, with a personal drawing power. He *sympathized*." She was a guitar player, and Ken told her he loved the music she made. He hoped someday to play a guitar in heaven. While listening to him preach, she heard the call of God to service, and although later she was tempted to forget the whole thing, Ken encouraged her by writing letters to her. "No matter where he was, nor how busy he was, he answered letters," she said.

"*La victoria se gana en el campo de batalla*. No salga," wrote Ken in one of those letters. "Victory is gained in the battlefield. Don't quit." He must himself have believed what he wrote. He then resolved to "quit bellyaching" to Elizabeth, or even to himself. He was in the battle, it was no time to quit, and like it or not he would stay. There were certain irreversible conditions which he was beginning to accept. He had always been touchy, for example, about his size. When a lady in California once asked him why Latins were so small he flared up and replied, "You don't realize that *most* of the world is small compared to North Americans!" Instead of allowing it to torment him for the rest of his life, he made up his mind to accept it as God's gift, and he preached a sermon on the text, "A Body Hast Thou Prepared for Me," which indicated his willingness to accept the gift. It might even prove to be the reason for some of his drive, he realized, and wrote, "Couldn't help wondering just how much of whatever drive I may have might be due to the fact that I am a little guy and unconsciously trying to compensate by getting somewhere in missions. Probably a lot more than I think, because constitutionally I am lazy and forever putting things off, and if I had been a six-footer I probably would have ended up being an athletic bum."

As to whether his own lack of what he sought—holiness—was to be regarded as irreversible he was not sure. He admitted that at times it did indeed seem so, yet at the same time he castigated himself for lack of faith. Surely there was something more to be had. How could he go on without it? "O for a meeting with the Lord which would permanently settle the matter!" he wrote, near the end of 1949.

1958. Left to right, front row: John, Kenneth, Elizabeth, Marie.
Standing: Robert, Cathy, Harry, Clare.

Last picture of Kenneth and Elizabeth together, 1964.

CHAPTER 11

It is, fortunately or unfortunately, nearly always possible to do without what we thought we could not do without. The meeting with the Lord had not yet taken place, but life went on. The Strachans began their tenth year of marriage in 1950. Elizabeth and the five children were in Ventnor, New Jersey, again in missionary apartments. Ken kept on traveling. He wondered about the future. "Sometimes it seems that it is all unreal. Sometimes I wish I could give more time to writing. Will we get settled in one place and have a home of our own? Will I have a study and books and become a writer? Or will it turn out to be a continuance of the past ten years?"

It was a continuance, and more. First he took an evangelistic trip to Guatemala. "Stark, mountainous terrain. . . . Indians trotting along mountain defiles. . . . A *pension* in cold Quezaltenango, then a flight down to Guatemala City . . . the indescribable beauty of Lake Atitlán surrounded by three volcanoes and with villages dotting the slopes and beach. Then the triangle of lofty volcanoes, Acatenango, Fuego, and Agua, and at their feet the ruins of Ciudad Vieja and Antigua. . . . For various reasons I had no burden for the message tonight—almost a sense of indifference—and I had more liberty than I've had all dry season. Can you explain it? One thing is clear —the experiences I've had thus far upset more than one theory I had about revival and campaign work, and thus far I'm not sure what are the correct answers." The questions—the upset theories—were not framed this time. Was it because Ken avoided articulating questions for which he had not at least a partial answer?

Then there was another trip to the States where the old temptations of material things—house, car, financial security—"have had such attraction to the extent of definitely draining me of spiritual life."

During the year of 1950 Ken again had an encounter which he took to be God's granting of his longtime prayer. This time it was at Indian Springs, Georgia, and he believed that he had at last been filled with the Holy Spirit. Whatever it was that had taken place in Greensboro, it seemed, had not lasted. But in Indian Springs, at an old-fashioned Wesleyan Methodist Campground, Ken went forward at the close of a meeting, seeking what they called "sanctification." On his way home from there he was driving along, singing, feeling very close to the Lord, when he came to an unmarked turn in the road and went over an embankment, completely demolishing the car, but escaping uninjured. He called Elizabeth, who went and got him, and on the way home he told her of his new experience with God. In an effort to make everything right with others as well as with God, he confessed to her a lie he had told her years before.

Eleven years later a letter Ken wrote to his son Harry revealed something of what he had learned through his repeated spiritual crises.

"I am sure—more than I have ever been in my life—that the Lord is faithful in keeping that which has been committed to Him, and that therefore He is at work in your life and will not let you go. Our tendency however is to feel that when we do drift away because of sin or coldness, that He turns His face too—but that is never so. You have years of fighting ahead of you and I'm praying that the Lord will keep you close to the source of victory—but I want you to know that regardless of what comes, He will never leave you, and neither will we. So don't let the consciousness of sin separate you from Him. It cannot, not since Calvary. That's the Devil's lie. *Nothing* can separate us from His love. (Isn't it strange how difficult it is to make words say what you want to say. And as I read this over it sounds so very trite to me, and I'm suddenly reminded that my own dad and mother wrote the same words to me thirty years ago and somehow failed to communicate with me then as I'm afraid I'll fail with you now.) But it doesn't matter, Harrucho, all I want to get over to you is the thought that the Lord will stick with you, and that in some less perfect way your dad and mother are also standing by."

In December Susan B. Strachan, Ken's mother, died. She had had several gall bladder attacks following her husband's death, but no one was quite prepared for the suddenness of her death. Ken was in the States when she became ill, and was unable to see her before she died. He soon submitted his resignation as co-director of the mission. The Board voted him into the full directorship and dreams of a quiet life on a little farm were scuttled once and for all.

He would arrive at his office in the mission buildings at seven o'clock in the morning and work until eleven-thirty, returning at two and staying until nearly six. Sometimes he worked in the evenings, sometimes on Saturdays. He tried to use a wire dictating machine but found mechanical things hopelessly confusing and went back to dictating to a secretary. He could break off in the middle of a letter and discuss things with her, for she was a person and not a machine. "He treated me like a person," she said later. "He was always a perfect gentleman, always kind." He trusted her to make corrections in grammar in his letters, but would write out his articles in long-hand, correct them himself, and ask a colleague or two to comment on them. An inveterate clipper of articles and quotations to be used in sermons or writings, Ken set up an elaborate filing system which eventually filled several large cabinets. When interrupted he gave no indication of resentment, though he preferred to have his door closed to discourage unnecessary intrusions. Sometimes his children came to visit or to "help" in the office. He would give them a small task and ask them to sit still and not talk.

To contemplate the nature and importance of his role seemed to have a heartening effect on Ken (though he once asked Elizabeth for advice on how to be absolutely convinced of the importance of what one was doing without becoming an "inflated bullfrog"). It was gratifying to know that the mission of which he was now the general director was, although a small one, well accepted in evangelical circles and constantly gaining favor.* Ken's attitude toward his position was a combination of deep pride for the heritage his re-

---

* By 1966 the LAM was one of eight missions which belonged to both the Interdenominational Foreign Mission Association of North America, Inc. and the Evangelical Foreign Missions Association. The former listed forty-four missions, the largest of which had 1,270 missionaries. The latter listed sixty-two missions, with 857 in the largest. The LAM claimed 144 missionaries in March, 1966.

spected parents had left him, and humility born of his own conviction that he could never live up to the powerful image of either parent. But after his mother's death he earnestly tried to fill the role she had vacated.

He visited the children at the orphanage farm and told them stories; he talked with the workers at the farm, not making any great attempts to inspire, as one said later, but "mainly trying to help us as together we stumbled along, trying to do more for the children"; he kept a list of the patients who were in the hospital and made a point of visiting at least those he knew; he investigated the progress of newly arrived missionaries in language school (he could be very stern—to one who had been reported cutting Spanish classes he issued the order, "You are *not to miss another class* unless you are so sick you can't walk there!"); and he kept up an always increasing correspondence, along with his regular work as preacher, teacher, director, and evangelist. The concept of "statesman" interested him, and he wrote out a list of the necessary qualifications:

"1) possesses certain strong guiding principles

"2) recognizes and keeps relationships

"3) prevision

"4) heart-power

"5) character ('Spending the morning writing a sonnet on virtue but spending the night in vice,' said of Lorenzo de Medici)

"6) cooperative spirit ('You may judge of the future outreach and influence of a nation by its capacity to cooperate with other nations,' Elihu Root)

"7) unselfishness ('He who would be first among you let him be the servant of all')

"8) courage."

An evangelistic campaign trip to Colombia, Venezuela, and Ecuador revived a sense of the original purpose of the Latin America Mission, and Ken visualized himself as a member of the team which would continue his father's work, reaching throughout Latin America. In Trinidad he attended services held by "Spiritual Baptists," a great crowd of black, shouting mumbo-jumbo followers. In Venezuela he met with Presbyterians and members of the Church of God. In Colombia with the Assemblies of God, in Ecuador with radio station HCJB, a "faith" mission for broadcasting the Gospel. From there he went south to Chile where he was overwhelmed at the visible success of the Pentecostal Church, and to Peru and Bolivia where he saw what the Methodists and Baptists had accomplished. If his hopes of joint campaigns, revivals, missionary retreats and ministerial conferences were to be realized he saw clearly that the primary requisite would be cooperation, an element notoriously lacking in Protestant missionary work in Latin America.

A new approach was needed, but if ever Ken felt like making no approach at all it was at this time. He was ill, and the doctor had prescribed a long rest. The family moved outside the city of San José to a town called Santo Domingo where Ken could be away from the telephone and the many demands which living in the Seminary entailed. His third daughter, Marie, had been born in August, and the house full of small children (Harry, now ten, was the oldest of six) could hardly provide the tranquillity which would have been ideal.

Early in 1952 he planned a campaign which included concerts by pianist Richard Foulkes and opera singer Anton Marco. Whatever else it was, this was a new approach, with these artists performing in concert halls and theaters in many large cities, often including in the program personal testimonies of their own experience of Jesus Christ. The concerts sometimes paved the way for Gospel meetings in the same halls, or provided opportunity to advertise meetings which would be held elsewhere in the city by the Latin America Mission.

The first campaign of this series was conducted in Managua, Nicaragua, and due to the illness of the evangelist Ken was asked to help. Things were not going as he believed they ought to be when he arrived, and when only six people responded to the invitation to accept Christ he returned to his hotel room bitterly discouraged. What was God trying to tell him? Surely He could do more than this. Had not the Lord granted him the special filling of the Spirit for which he had prayed? What was to be the fruit of this special gift? Perhaps God had brought Ken to Managua for an unusual purpose. Ken began to pray. Not that he felt that there was anything he himself could do. If anything was done it would have to be God who did it. Had not God led the way in the commencement of these campaigns? Had He not guided, years before, in the very founding of the mission for this purpose? Was He to be glorified in these pitifully meager results? Ken could not believe that He was, and as he prayed he became convinced that God did indeed intend to do something, something visible and tangible and demonstrable for the glory of His name. He would, in the first place, grant good weather so that the people would come out to the meetings. In the second place, He would save fifty souls. But He would be *asked* for those two things, and someone must exercise the necessary faith for the asking.

Ken accepted the challenge. He prayed that it would not rain, and that fifty souls would be saved in the closing night of the campaign. What was his amazement and glee to learn the next day that the evangelist who was ill in the hospital had been given faith to ask for precisely the same things. This must be it. Ken went confidently to the meeting, and although it looked like rain, he assured his audience that God would hold it off until He had "won a great victory." The people listened to his pronouncement with one ear, and to the thunder which was coming closer with the other. The thunder was the more convincing sound as it soon brought with it torrents of rain and within minutes the crowd had dissolved. With it Ken's hopes dissolved too. There had been failures in the Nicaragua campaign— some of them could be attributed to improper planning, some to lack of dedication or sanctification on the part of those responsible, some perhaps to Satan himself. What could be said of a rain storm which drove away the entire congregation, including the fifty marked out by faith for a decision of life-and-death importance? To which of the possible causes could such a storm be assigned? Ken knew only one answer, and it was not one that was comfortable or reassuring. It is God who makes the rain to fall, on the just and on the unjust. It was God who gave Elijah the faith to pray that it might not rain, and it did not rain. It was God, Strachan believed, who had given him the faith to pray for the same thing. It was God who alone could answer the prayer. And it was God who caused it to rain, who dashed cold water in their faces.

Several times in later years Strachan told this story publicly. Once when asked to speak on the subject of prayer he used this story of his own experience. It was utterly baffling to him, and he admitted this. It seems that he simply accepted it as one of God's mysteries, but there was no explanation of the promise he thought he had been given, or of the prayer of faith which, according to Scripture, will be answered. "If ye ask anything in My name," said Jesus, "I will do it."

An editorial appeared in the May/June issue of the *Evangelist* that year called "Greener Pastures." Ken wrote of the human desire for the grass on the other side of the fence. He cited the Bible story of Abraham and Lot, gazing over the valley where they were to work. Lot chose the one with the green grass, Abraham stayed where he was. "By faith he sojourned." The article closes with the verse from the Twenty-third Psalm, "He maketh me to lie down in green pastures," and with two admonitions from St. Paul: "Be content," and "Be ye steadfast."

No one knew better than Ken his own need for such stabilizing words. He saw in himself Lot's materialism and faithlessness, the discontent which seeks another way than the one appointed. Only a month later he wrote that he felt "like Jonah, wanting to get away from everything and from all responsibility," and it is as though his writing and preaching were always for himself, first of all. It was perhaps this frank humanness which lent more weight to his words than if he had paraded a great strength and example.

Again during the summer he was ill, first with vague aches and pains and cramps, then with something which simulated heart trouble and necessitated another rest away from home. By October he had gone to the States and checked into a hospital for a thorough physical examination. There were no medical findings other than fatigue and overwork, and he was discharged with orders to rest for two more months.

Elizabeth had stayed behind in San José, and received word from her husband instructing her to sell the piano, the car, the refrigerator, and the children's bicycles, pack up their things and move herself and the six children to the United States. She did it. Not that Ken entertained a moment's doubt that she would do it. That it might be *difficult* to carry out these instructions singlehanded probably did not occur to him. He was in high spirits when he met her plane in Miami, and failed to comprehend her lack of enthusiasm when he proposed whizzing her out for an evening on the town.

Most of the next two years were spent in the United States, with the usual traveling and speaking, punctuated by periods with the family, sometimes in ill health, sometimes working on his favorite indoor project of formulating principles and policies for the family, for his personal life, or for the mission. He loved to work out propositions for the work of the mission, his own relationships with people, his own or the mission's objectives, witnessing for Christ, or whatever idea seemed to be in need of revamping. He asked Elizabeth to do the same. His files are loaded with sheets and slips and scraps of paper with numbered lists, outlines, diagrams.

The LAM, like most other North America-based missionary organizations, was operated on the principles of the business corporation. This was not always acknowledged or even recognized, for it was generally thought of only as Christian work, or the Lord's work, and hence not subject to the same conditions as a corporation. There was, however, a board of directors with a carefully organized system of departments, each with its own hierarchy of officials. There were annual meetings of the directors, of the field council, of the mission "family," and annual conferences in the United States, which anyone interested (this usually included some of the financial backers) might attend. The home director would make an annual report to the general directors, which included the number of times he had spoken as a representative of the mission, the number of meetings attended, the number of dollars received, potential recruits interviewed, "prayer partners" enlisted, and the results of seminary graduates' work overseas. He added a list of churches which he considered "especially ripe for cultivation by the LAM," and a second list where "I just do not feel that we need to send any further representation."

Promotion was an area in which Ken himself, in spite of his often expressed distaste for and suspicion of the whole principle, did a great deal of thinking and planning. He recommended that the mission place more emphasis on strategic position (there was no other "service organization" dedicated to reaching the whole of Latin America), experience (the mission was older than most other non-denominational missions on the continent), and reputation (the names of Harry and Susan Strachan opened doors). Success, on the other hand, Ken was careful to remind the board, would depend entirely on the "Lord's hand upon us," "our sense of mission," "our deep conviction that the biggest work is ahead." Any past successes were looked upon as "remarkable tokens of the Lord's dealings, and confirmation of His leading."

A basic requirement of Christian promotion, wrote Ken, was that it glorify God. "We must resist the temptation to grab some of the glory for the organization we are promoting. Our deputation messages, our prayer letters, our promotional literature must all be characterized by the presence of that which glorifies God. We must avoid the subtle brand of pseudo-humility which angles for praise and honor." It is small wonder that the convolutions of this task—working out a method of promotion for the LAM which would not promote the LAM so much as it glorified God—caused Ken to wish now and then for the wings of a dove, that he might fly away and be at rest.

The idea of a corporate image was an important one, and Ken emphasized that in order to preserve it, there must be strict adherence to the mission rule of no "direct" solicitation of funds. Members must, rather, reflect a "cheerful confidence in the Lord without hypocrisy," but he then added that the bearing of this regulation upon the customary use of postpaid return envelopes in mission literature ought to be reconsidered in the next meeting of the home council. In another of Ken's "memos" to colleagues, of which he wrote hundreds of pages in his lifetime, are queries as to how the rigid LAM policies of "no debts" and "no direct solicitation" might be modified to allow some latitude. Was there a way of soliciting indirectly, for example, which would not affect the image nor alienate the constituency, and at the same time demonstrate their "cheerful confidence in the Lord without hypocrisy"? There must, he further stated, be no specific commitments on projects, no announced financial goals, for "God Himself will provide (Matthew 6:6, 'Thy father which seeth in secret shall reward thee openly')." Lest the financial and promotional policies be misunderstood Ken explained, "This is not to suggest that we discontinue or diminish our promotional activities—it is rather to suggest a reorientation which will permit an intensified promotional program that we believe will be more to the glory of God."

Ken had reached the "top," as it were, in his own world, and was paying a high price in his health and the continual sacrifice of his family in order to stay there. In this he was not different from those in other fields who also reach the top. Sir Laurence Olivier, the great actor, said, "Once you get to the top, the load of staying there is almost superhuman. And you feel so tired sometimes of the responsibility—the various efforts that have to be made not to let yourself down, not to let other people down, not to let the theater in general down. And there are periods in actors' lives when they fall completely out of tune with their art. . . . If you're not in the mood, you have to employ all the technique you've ever learnt in order to achieve a certain voltage very quickly."

Missionaries are, of course, human. Ken was human. He would have sympathized with Olivier. One of the more significant differences between them, aside from the enormous difference in the nature of their fields, was that Ken believed himself to have been specially called by God, raised to the top by God, and engaged in a work which could be accomplished, not by "various efforts . . . not to let yourself down," not by techniques calculated to achieve a certain voltage, not by art or ability or education or human energy of any kind, but "by my Spirit, saith the Lord." This was the one condition of success, and so far as Ken could see, this was the one condition not fulfilled. He might struggle along, the victim of many moods and tempers, he might recognize only too clearly his own limitations and weaknesses, he might put forth nearly superhuman efforts to work above his feelings and the circumstances which seemed to conspire to defeat him, but he knew it was a fruitless task unless God Himself stepped in and made it fruitful. And Ken always looked for this intervention in terms of something done in or to him personally. "Sometimes I feel that I cannot continue to carry the responsibility of the mission unless the Lord does something special for me," he wrote in October, 1953. This was after he had twice received by faith the gift of the Holy Spirit. It was one thing for a business man or an actor or a general or an athlete to expect to succeed by his own efforts. He might have troubles of many kinds and have to make sacrifices, but it was his own game, and he was in it for himself. Strachan could not believe that the mission was in the same category. It was doing spiritual work, and had therefore a claim to special help from God. He saw God's hand at work in a thousand ways—provision of his own temporal needs, the comfort of the Scriptures in times of depression, the gift of a lovely wife and children, guidance in daily affairs, harmonious relationships among missionaries, souls saved through the various avenues of the work, an ever-expanding influence for the LAM in Latin America—these he gladly acknowledged as gifts from God. He still believed, however, that he should personally experience the peace and joy and rest and confidence of the true Christian, and could not operate indefinitely without them. Should he resign as General Director? Was it honest for him to retain such a role when it did not "feel real" to him? There is no indication anywhere in his writings that he found a satisfactory answer to these questions. Perhaps it was not necessary or even possible for Ken Strachan to "feel real." He had moments when he did feel "called," or "destined." He had also moments— few and brief but nonetheless lucid—when he questioned the authenticity of his definition of missionary work. Aloud, he would affirm positively his conviction that the primary aim was right, and that the LAM was by divine commission directly promoting that aim. It was this public conviction and the ability to vocalize it, as well as his status in the LAM, which earned him recognition as a missionary leader and creative thinker, and he was invited to address a group of mission executives at a retreat in Wisconsin in 1954. What he said there touched lightly and cautiously upon some of his private questioning. If thoroughly understood and applied, it might have revolutionized the American Protestant view of foreign missions. That he could say it and still maintain his position among them is perhaps some indication of the evangelical's ability to swallow a camel.

"We have reached a point where we can no longer consider that the chief answer to world-wide evangelism is to be found in the sending forth and support of foreign missionaries. . . . It could well be that as far as the missionary task of the Church is concerned, the emphasis might swing from the missionary society as a separate, specialized organization back to the Church itself." He went on to speak of the need to establish indigenous churches with competent national leaders supported by the congregations themselves. He recognized the difficulty of promoting this idea in churches in the United States. "The cry has been for more missionaries and more support for missionaries. Promotionally speaking, no other appeal has been so effective in presenting the cause of missions to the home constituency. . . . But we may not be entirely right in the deduction which we unconsciously make that the chief medium of world evangelism is the American missionary. As a matter of fact, one of the problems which societies are already beginning to face is that of reaching a saturation point as far as the number of foreign workers which can be stationed advantageously in a given area." He pointed out that up until that time two separate establishments had been operating on the foreign field: the indigenous church and the foreign organization. "We like to picture it as the building and the scaffolding. But what an imposing scaffolding! Scaffold upon scaffold, girders to support girders, and how small a building over which it towers." One of his colleagues in the LAM likened it to a scaffold of gold supporting a house of straw.

The solution, Ken said, would not be easy to find. "It may demand that the temptation to stress that which appeals most to the sentiment of the home constituency be resisted. Such stock-in-trade as the dramatic appeal for the foreign missionary and over-emphasized generalizations on the poverty and backwardness of the benighted peoples across the sea may have to be abandonned for the sake of presenting a realistic picture of the modern world outside of Christ and acquainting the church at home with its true situation and the sober demands thereof. . . . Some way must be found to bring the national church and its leaders into partnership in the planning and execution of *all missionary*, not merely church, endeavor."

This was the beginning, for the Latin America Mission, of an effort toward this partnership, called Latinamericanization—an assimilation of Latin Americans into the organization and the gradual transformation of the society into a service agency of and for the Latin American church.

In Ken's file was a section labeled "Latinamericanization." In this section was the following story:

Colonel Lawrence Van der Post, a South African novelist and soldier, was asked by a Dutchman what was the explanation of why the Indonesians, after World War II had asked the Dutch to get out of their country. The Dutchman said, "We built up their country, brought in industry, lifted the people to a higher level of life and of living standards, and increased their span of living. Then they ask us to go! Why?" The Colonel's reply: "The look in your eye. You did not look at the Indonesians with compassion, but condescension, not with sympathy but superiority, not admiration but arrogance, not pity but pride, not graciousness but greed, not to give but to get, and your true inner attitude came out through the look in your eye."

CHAPTER 12

One of Strachan's friends said of him that he loved not only children but the *idea* of children. He had mentioned offhandedly in one of his courtship letters to Elizabeth that he thought perhaps a half dozen children would do, provided they did not make too much noise. It is doubtful that the Strachan children were less noisy than most, but their father was crazy about them, and a "subtle braggart," as another friend said, whenever he found opportunity to mention them. In his role as a father, both his wife and children rated him "A-plus." Harry believed, for a part of his tender years, that Daddy had actually made the stars. Ken once stated that if he had to choose between having his children's respect and having their love he would prefer their respect. It seems he had both.

His frequent absences from home gave him a certain aura. It was Mother who day after day had to impose discipline and maintain order. It was Mother who washed faces and fed tots in highchairs and asked if teeth had been brushed and beds made and Bibles read and homework done and pianos practiced. It was Father who wrote cute letters home to his children, promising them "the biggest banana split in San José when I get home," telling them he was proud of them, asking if they wanted him as a Daddy still, "or would you rather find another?" When they learned he was coming home, there would be great excitement and a joyful countdown—five more days, four more days, three more, two, . . . Then a grand excursion to the airport, hugs and kisses for each one, a gala "Welcome Home" supper that night, the promised treats and presents. But his youngest child, Marie, sensed that "he was always full of worries.

But my friends loved him, and he was always nice to them, played with them and joked with them. But I sometimes thought he was almost too worried to really have fun."

He was interested in his children's grades in school, their little money-making schemes, their hobbies and projects. He tried to instill into each one a warm sense of family oneness. "Love each other, help each other, stick together as a family," he wrote to them, and one of his sons said, "He gave me tools for becoming a person, for finding myself. Perhaps some of the tools were useless, but he did give me one good one: basic family love."

He liked the idea of having family worship together, and sometimes there would be days in a row when it was held regularly, with each one participating in Bible reading and memorization, followed by prayer. But any sort of rigid routine was distasteful to Ken and there would be gaps, sometimes because his schedule did not permit time with the family, but more often because it was too complicated to get them all together and quiet in one place, or because he himself did not feel inclined to make the effort to do so.

Usually Ken and Elizabeth presented a united front on matters regarding the children, but occasionally a child, sensing that his father's views were more liberal in some areas, approached him first and was told to do whatever he liked. "Oh no, Ken, he shouldn't!" Elizabeth would protest, and then would follow a discussion in which Ken usually came around to his wife's position. He took the view that she, after all, had the principal burden of rearing the children and probably knew how to do a better job than he did. He was very insistent on one thing: his sons were to respect their mother and sisters. If chivalry were dead, Ken Strachan was determined to resurrect it in his sons. "If I ever catch you hitting a girl I'll knock your brains out," he told his son Robin. Elizabeth had a somewhat gentler approach, according to Harry: "Mother would bust up a fight and send each of us to our own room with the admonition that we couldn't come out until we had asked and received from God love in our hearts for whomever we had been pounding on the nose minutes earlier." "Yes, Johnny," wrote Ken while away on a trip, "You *must* love your sisters!"

The children understood that their father was the lord of his own castle. When he was at home, life revolved around him, and "nobody except Daddy was *allowed* to have headaches or allergies or be picky about food." Ken's tastes were not exotic, but he did have a somewhat temperamental stomach, and greatly appreciated good food, well prepared. Elizabeth found it difficult to take so ephemeral a matter as the daily menu very seriously, and on one occasion, according to a story which has varied versions, she served up one of her casseroles which she called "Old Friends," consisting, one daughter alleges, of left-over noodles, tomatoes, and some unidentified ingredient which "looked, tasted, and felt like oatmeal" all covered with cheese for camouflage. Ken was the first to venture a mouthful of this creation. "Elizabeth, you can't expect us to eat this," he said. Then, to the children, "I'm going to shut my eyes and count to ten. You can do anything you want with your food," whereupon the family rose from the table in a body, carried their plates and scraped them into the garbage pail. In a letter Ken once suggested that Elizabeth might give a little more thought to the evening meal. She obeyed, and in later letters he commended her for it. The budget she was required to adhere to was undoubtedly one factor in determining what appeared on the table, but Ken was hardly aware of this angle until the fall of 1955 when Elizabeth was the one who went away and Ken stayed home to care for the children. They demonstrated for him how thoroughly she had been doing her job. He wrote that they were "simply marvelous, with a minimum of scrapping and maximum of singing and playing together." Instead of letters reporting on the number of meetings he had spoken in or the visits made, Ken wrote this time about Clare's loose tooth and the children's shoes needing mending. "How much am I to pay the ironing girl?" "I'll never let you go again." "Don't know if I can hold out for four more weeks." He exceeded the budget in his spending and had to borrow money from his children to pay grocery bills. He washed dishes, carefully pulling the blinds beforehand lest any Costa Rican see him thus in disgrace, performing a woman's task.

Some who knew Ken called him a visionary; others said he was not a visionary but a very practical, down-to-earth administrator. Ken himself had written to Elizabeth years before that he had much sympathy for Joseph who was called by his brothers a dreamer. "I

like men whose vision carries them far beyond their own horizons."
One of his Latin colleagues said of him, "He was always ahead of
us, thinking." His understanding of the need for indigenous church
principles was at least ten years in advance of average evangelical
thinking, and once in the 1950's, while serving on the board of
another faith mission, he was consulted on the appointment of a
Negro worker. He stated his strong conviction that race should not
be a consideration. In this he was virtually alone at that time, though
a few years later only a minority would have been surprised at such
an opinion. This represented a long step from his attitude while a
student in Dallas, when he had written patronizingly of the southern
Negroes whom he saw in the city, or whose churches he occasionally
attended. He believed so thoroughly in racial equality that he eventually became a member of the National Association for the Ad-
vancement of Colored People.

He loved to stand on a hilltop outside of San José and watch the
sunset, or drive up into the mountains at night to see the panorama
of twinkling lights below. From a hotel balcony in Colombia he
wrote of looking out over a broad beach to the ocean and seeing two-
masted sailboats loaded with coconuts. From a river boat in the
jungle of Colombia he wrote of the "late afternoon sun over large
expanses of swamp lakes, cloud formations, bright green beds of
swamp grass, dark green of trees, blue of hills, grey and blue and
pink of sky, birds flying and singing."

In his imagination too he loved to look out over panoramas of the
fields of service where his mission was operating, and of possibilities
for the future. In the *Evangelist* for September/November, 1955, he
outlined the aims of the Latin America Mission:

"1) to evangelize the continent
"2) to build the church
"3) to train the leadership
"4) to demonstrate the Gospel.

"This is a brief summary of our work. But it does not do justice to
it. It does not picture as we long to do the multitudes in bursting
cities, the unreached towns and villages, the seas of upturned faces
in campaign meetings, young Latin Americans at study in Institute
and Seminary, nurses and doctors in surgery and free clinic, children

studying God's word, congregations meeting, chapels going up, all the behind-the-scenes activities that hurl the Gospel out over the air, literature, written, printed, and placed in eager hands. It does not picture a staff of around three hundred (a Gideon's three hundred, we trust), each with his separate ability and ministry, each in need of prayer for the battle."

Ken had the ability to see potential in individuals, often a potential which they themselves did not see, and to draw them into places where that potential could be realized. He sometimes went too far, and placed more confidence in people than they deserved, but this was, in the eyes of one fellow worker, "a very small failing." Indeed, it is difficult to find a single Latin who knew him well who can think of any faults Ken had. There are Latin Americans who are ministers and missionaries today because Ken Strachan "found" them, encouraged them, and gave them a place to work. Juan Isais, Jonás Gonzalez, and Victor Monterroso are among the men in whom Strachan recognized potential, whom he helped in countless ways, and to whom he ultimately delegated large responsibilities in the work of the mission.

He was glad that his two closest associates in the management of the LAM were men of extreme practicality and business sense. Dayton Roberts was his brother-in-law, and Horace (always called Dit) Fenton was a friend from Wheaton days whom Ken had tried to persuade to join the mission. After several years Fenton was convinced, as Ken had been for some time, that this was God's call. Mother Strachan had told her son-in-law that he must try to keep Ken's feet on the ground, and at times when Ken's vision took him beyond reason or reality Dit and Dayton acted as reins or "plodders," as they called themselves. One occasion when Ken was carried beyond all bounds was the annual mission meeting of December, 1955. It was his custom to present a general director's report, and this time he made it in the form of a prophecy. "Let me try to peep into the immediate future and visualize the LAM's outreach and activities ten years from now.

"As we drive along the beautiful four-lane highway from El Coco's magnificent airport straight into the heart of the city, we are overwhelmed by the growth of San José. Its population now is reaching close to 300,000 [in 1965 it had reached that figure] and two throughways bisect the heart of the city [no throughway had been completed by 1965]. The main center seems to have grown upwards three or four stories and is completely modernized. A quick tour brings added joy as we pass the Templo Bíblico, now a three-story building with its main auditorium seating fifteen hundred and its Sunday School attendance running over a thousand. [In 1965 the average attendance was 450.] . . .

"In the Northeast section a main thoroughfare brings us quickly to the beautiful grounds of the evangelical school where some 600 children [in 1965 enrollment was 275] are enrolled. . . .

"The Colegio Nocturno Evangélico uses the same buildings. [This was a dream unrealized by 1965.]

"The LAM's staff has more than doubled, and now numbers close to five hundred in Costa Rica alone. [By 1965 there were 275]

"VIDA, the popular evangelical magazine, after a struggle of several years, is now in the black and its circulation has just recently gone over the 100,000 mark. [By 1965 this had been taken over by another mission and had a circulation of about 30,000.]

"We are soon sitting in the office of the field director, listening to the story of the Mission's growth during the past few years. He speaks English with remarkable facility, in spite of his accent. . . ."

The prophecy included anti-Protestant pressures in the Colombia field, overwork for some of the missionaries which resulted in a threatened split, spiritual dryness, criticism from other missionary societies, and a covenant of prayer which led to lowered tensions, improved health, increase in financial support, visible results in the work. A vow of total renunciation resulted in unity, love, and loyalty between workers and a monthly day of prayer and fasting. It would be nearly impossible to gauge the accuracy of these last predictions. There may have been lowered tensions, improved health for some. The year 1965 was the year of Ken's death. There was, by that time, a monthly day of prayer. As for the other things Ken saw in his prophecy, who can measure them?

"I do not think that I have been overoptimistic," Ken added. "As a matter of fact . . . I think that my prophecy may very well have been unduly conservative. In any case, please do not hold me to it ten years from now. In the course of my imaginings I was tempted to draw into the picture a slightly stout, white-haired retired missionary put out to pasture and thus disclaim any responsibility for the developments which had transpired.

"In this paper my hope has been in some poor way to stimulate our faith and vision for the future and my prayer that the Lord might make each of us willing to pay the price for that fuller and more fruitful ministry which I believe He would have us experience in the next ten years. God grant that it may be so."

Ken's concept of "Latinamericanization" was the basis for his hopes of expansion, and early in the year 1956 he embarked on a campaign with the Latin American evangelist Juan Isais, to Cuba, Jamaica, the Dominican Republic, Puerto Rico, and the Virgin Islands. Again he was accompanied by singer Anton Marco and a pianist, Bill Herzog. The idea had come to him that an intensive campaign with evangelist Billy Graham would be enormously effective at this juncture, and he exhausted himself visiting, preaching, interviewing evangelical leaders and seminary alumni, paying courtesy calls on officials, and attempting to feel out the possibilities for inviting Graham to come to the Caribbean.

On April 17 he wrote to Elizabeth from St. Thomas:

"On the whole I feel satisfied with the trip thus far. . . . On the other hand, dear, this trip has been a hard one as far as my state of mind and soul have been concerned. At times I have even wondered whether the passages in Hebrews 6 and 10 and 12:17 [references to the impossibility of repentance for those who have rejected the truth] were not descriptive of my present situation after the touches from the Lord that I had experienced a few years back. As far as understanding the secret of a happy Christian life, or the perfect law of liberty or the victorious life or sanctification or whatever you want to call it—I'm more uncertain than ever. I oscillate between feelings of desperation and feelings of complete indifference and at all times am subject to carnal and rebellious thoughts. At times when I can pray, my prayer is that the Lord will do a work in me, a filling of the Spirit that will put me on a new plane of life and service—not necessarily one of immunity from testing and suffering, but one of new strength and faith and stability in following the Lord completely and in meeting the challenges of life.

"This affects my relationship to you, dear, and to the children—
and that's why my letters thus far have been so few and poor. I
know that I love you. . . . I just love the children and am so proud of
each one of them, and feel that all the credit for what they are goes
to you. And they represent—as you so often remark—six tremendous reasons for wanting to live and for wanting to be true. But that
doesn't tackle or solve that inner conflict between that ugly self that
is me and that other self that recognizes that he can never be fully
happy or successful until he is fully committed to the Lord and loves
Him with the whole heart and mind and strength. . . .

"I have been fighting all along with a self that is essentially
sensual and earthly and that has never been fully surrendered no
matter how many times I've tried to be. . . . Whether I can ever be
wholly and completely the Lord's, or whether the pattern of my life
has already been frozen is the big question of my life. And if it's the
latter I don't know how I can go on preaching about the power of
the Gospel, since the only alternatives are then: either the Gospel is
limited by human limitations of appropriation or else RKS having
tasted the power of the Gospel and fallen away can no longer experience its power in his life."

Granted the premises from which he argued, Strachan's logic
was ineluctable. He had defined for himself the corner into which
he had been backed, and yet he somehow went doggedly on, unable
to silence the arguments, unable also to take any other position.
In Dostoevski's *The Brothers Karamazov* a lady comes to the old Father Zossima in despair because of her spiritual state. He says to her,
"Love in action is a harsh and dreadful thing compared with love in
dreams. Love in dreams is greedy for immediate action, rapidly
performed and in the sight of all. Men will even give their lives if
only the ordeal does not last long but is soon over, with all looking
on and applauding as though on the stage. But active love is labor
and fortitude, and for some people, too, perhaps, a complete science.
But I predict that just when you see with horror that in spite of all
your efforts you are getting further from your goal instead of nearer
to it—at that very moment I predict that you will reach it and
behold clearly the miraculous power of the Lord who has been all
the time loving and mysteriously guiding you." Perhaps if Ken
Strachan had had such a wise and loving counselor he might have

been enabled to look on his position from a different perspective.

In May he went to Richmond, Virginia, where Billy Graham was holding an evangelistic campaign. During a twenty-minute ride in a motorcade with Graham, Ken asked if he would be willing to come to Latin America. He said he would, and Ken returned home to plan and pray.

A single sheet of paper, written in red ink and blotted here and there, seems to contain the seed thought of a new missionary endeavor, that which became known throughout Latin America in Ken's lifetime, and in many other parts of the world after his death, as "Evangelism-in-Depth." On the paper he had written:

"Planning Future Work:

"Tie in campaigns and all our ministries to a drive country by country to *finish* the job of evangelism.

"Prepare by making a survey of the unreached towns and villages and rural areas (including Indian)—then seek to enlist all local evangelical forces in a prolonged campaign to bring an effective witness to that area. Bring in a *team* to that country, set up a temporary headquarters, map out a plan of campaign, stress personal evangelism and *train* for it and for follow-up; carry out series of evangelistic efforts in strategic areas, utilize radio, literature, child evangelism; carry out simultaneous training program in churches for lay workers, etc."

In August Ken was back in the States, having to have medical examinations again. He had been troubled with gastritis, which the doctors said had been aggravated by the tensions of traveling and meetings. Ken wrote to his wife, "I am ready to settle down for keeps. No more travelling for me!" On second thought he was not sure he ought to make such a pronouncement, and asked her if she thought the time had come when "without presumption I could figure on staying put in one place and arrange so that others do the traveling?"

It was while he was in New York seeing the doctors that Ken suddenly realized how the years were passing and he had not done what he intended to do for the children. Harry had already been away in boarding school for a year and Cathy would soon be leaving also. The time Ken spent at home with the others was decreasing rather than increasing, and he wanted to make the best of it from now on. He went out and bought a record-player and some records: music, poetry reading, Peter Marshall's sermons. His mission, its organization and administration, its enormous objective of the total evangelization of Latin America—and the thousand activities which pressed daily upon this harassed man—were they, after all, of paramount importance? Was he to supervise the winning of nations and leave the nurture of his own children solely in his wife's hands? No—he did not want that. Neither did he want his children, as they grew up, to go astray on that point. He sat down and wrote in a letter to Harry: "People are always more important than things or accomplishments, and the Lord Himself is more important than anything. That's the end of the sermon, son. I love you, and we'll take up no offering."

The year 1957 began with the annual mission meetings in Colombia, after which Ken visited again the little town where he had preached his sermon on Christian Discipline years before. "Dogs—at least a half dozen of them, barking their fool heads off, a baby bawling on the street just outside the paper-thin partition of my room, a radio blaring out the usual Latin American jazz, a burro blowing his top—it's terrific. I've just had a bath a la calabash bowl and am going to sleep under a mosquito net now."

Elizabeth's circular letter of February records, "Ken has just come back from five weeks in Colombia, and he was thrilled with the wonderful blessing there in spite of limitations and persecutions. The lay believers are out evangelizing after the manner of the early Church."

Preparations for the Billy Graham meetings to be held in 1958 occupied his time for the rest of the year. From Puerto Rico he wrote that he had spent most of the time "on my feet, trying to dodge the pitfalls of cooperation." This became one of his chief preoccupations. It was essential that Christians forget their minor differences and unite in recognition of their major concerns. His own convictions were subjected to a difficult test when a Pentecostalist arrived in San José to hold revival meetings and sought the endorsement and cooperation of the Latin America Mission. Ken found himself in an indefinable position. Here was a man trying to do

exactly what Strachan had been trying to do—bring Christians together for a united evangelistic campaign. But, like many of the
pastors and leaders whom Ken had talked with in Puerto Rico and
other countries, Ken had certain reservations about the wisdom of
cooperating in this effort. He had always been strangely drawn to
Pentecostalism, sometimes slipping away secretly while on a visit to
another city and attending their meetings instead of the churches of
his hosts. There was in him the suspicion—even the hope—that they
might, after all, be more right than he had been led to believe. They
perhaps "had something"—was it not evidenced by strange tokens
and signs?—and it might be what he himself was so desperately
seeking. He had copied into his notebook and quoted on several
occasions a statement from Bishop Lesslie Newbigin: "The living
Spirit can and does give His own life to bodies which lack in some
manner and measure the fullness of the Church's true order and
teaching. When He does so . . . we must 'hold our peace and glorify
God.' There can be no evasion of this, no suggestion that we can
acknowledge the presence of the Holy Spirit and yet deny the fullest
Christian fellowship, as though our church rules were stricter than
those of God Himself."

Did Strachan not comprehend the full implication of Newbigin's
categorical statement? Did he not think it applicable in this instance?
Was the test too difficult? He did not like to oppose the revival
meetings, but he liked less to assume the public risk of identifying
himself and his mission with them. To "hold his peace and glorify
God" in this case did not seem to him the thing to do. Instead he
entertained the leaders of the Pentecostal group at coffee, welcomed
them, and explained as kindly as he could his inability to go along
with them because of their "undue emphasis on healing in the atone-
ment." A question had been raised (Ken did not call it heresy or
false teaching) and he felt he had answered it. There must have been
those on the other side for whom his answer was an evasion, who
felt that, after all, he had indeed "denied them the fullest Christian
fellowship," and that the rules of the LAM were "stricter than those
of God Himself." Ken would of course have protested that they were
God's own rules, and both sides undoubtedly found in their hymnals
Frederick W. Faber's words,

But we make His love too narrow
By false limits of our own,
And we magnify its strictness
With a zeal He will not own.

The sequel to the story: there was a campaign in the bull ring, the government closed it and imprisoned the evangelist on the charge that it was unsafe to have so many sick people in one place. Ken saw the subterfuge and led a protest which resulted in the release of the prisoner.

Ken was one of the first Fundamentalists ever to be invited to address a conference sponsored by the National Council of Churches of Christ. At Buck Hill Falls, Pennsylvania, in 1957 he made a plea for recognition of and cooperation with "the nonhistorical groups" in Latin America, those missionary enterprises not officially linked with the traditional denominations. "The future of evangelical work in Latin America is intimately bound up with theirs."

His "ministry of reconciliation" was not confined to efforts to bridge the chasms between denominations. On an intimate, personal level he tried to strengthen and preserve relationships. When a co-worker was contemplating divorce Ken listened long and carefully to his story, trying to find the truth and the solution, stunned and sad to think of such a breach in the life of his friend, and of its effects on the work they were doing together. He wrote a letter, assuring the man of his sympathy and prayer. "I have tried to put myself in your situation. I recognize how difficult it is. How can one go on in a matrimonial situation which apparently has become intolerable? Humanly speaking it is perhaps impossible. Might God work a miracle? . . . This is the biggest crisis in your life, brother, and I pray God to give you the courage to choose the right way. It is not necessary to remind you that you can count on my love. I will keep on praying. . . . If you can believe, with God all things are possible." After a time, a long journey and further conversation were necessary, but the man decided in the end to remain with his wife.

In June Ken and Elizabeth went together to Wheaton, Illinois, the scene throughout the bleakest years of his life of so many academic and spiritual struggles and defeats. This time his alma mater granted him an honorary degree of Doctor of Letters.

In August Billy Graham invited him to appear on the platform with him in Madison Square Garden to announce, before seventeen thousand people, the forthcoming Latin America campaign.

What if the campaign should be a failure? Ken spent the next months in a fever of planning and liaison work throughout the Caribbean. It was God's work he was doing, he believed, and he thoroughly believed that Billy Graham was God's man. There was no doubt in his mind that Latin America was desperately in need of the message Graham had to give. It remained only for him—Ken Strachan—and his colleagues to lay the groundwork for the meetings. Here was the rub. If the whole thing was a flop who would there be to blame? God? Billy Graham? Very unlikely.

Ken's health suffered again, and he participated in a student missionary conference in Illinois with an upset stomach "almost the entire time." The family suffered. "I feel that I have neglected the children. Please tell them it's been because of the rush of things, and I'll try to be a better daddy to them when all is over."

The Graham campaign in Venezuela had to be canceled at the last minute because of political unrest. In Puerto Rico and the British Islands of Jamaica, Barbados, and Trinidad, it was such a success that Ken was able to relax a little, but his health was in so precarious a state that the doctors advised him to find a place where he could live quietly. While he was engaged in the campaigns Elizabeth looked for such a place. After much difficulty and many prayers she found it—a long, low, rambling ranch house set in a garden on a hillside overlooking the great valley called the Meseta Central. It was almost the dream house Ken had longed for since his youth, "a little place to call our own," "an island where I can build a hut and plant a garden and take the girl of my dreams." There was a brick terrace with a duck pond below; there was a separate little chalet at the bottom of the garden where Ken could be completely alone for study and writing; there was a huge living room with broad windows looking out on the mountains; there were six bedrooms—space, for the first time in their lives, for all the family to live and breathe easily.

February to July of 1958 was an oasis. Ken had been given freedom to live and work quietly at the new place and he was grateful for it. The mission had asked him to write a history of the

LAM and the story of his parents' lives. He also took up poultry-raising and visualized other projects which would satisfy his hankering to be a farmer. But in July he was gone again, to Nicaragua for meetings, and then to speak in summer conferences in the States. Elizabeth had carefully made out a list of things she and the children needed which were not available in Costa Rica. Ken wrote that he had lost the list and sizes.

When he came home, it was to take time off for contemplation on things learned during the Graham crusade and on the future of the LAM's evangelistic method. The Partnership Program of the mission, also called Latinamericanization, had succeeded to a degree. The Billy Graham crusade had proved that many different kinds of Christians were capable of cooperating in a single effort to propogate their message. Ken had thought for a long time about the Scripture which says, "He that soweth sparingly shall reap also sparingly," and wondered if there were not a more effective sowing technique than they had hitherto hit upon. He began to study the reasons for the success of various churches, sects, and ideologies, and concluded that "the growth of any movement is in direct proportion to the ability of that movement to mobilize its total membership in the constant propogation of its beliefs."

It was here that Ken made the most critical choice of his life. Would he do the thing he longed to do, stop traveling, learn to be quiet, give time to his family, live healthily and happily on the farm, and try to be a shepherd with his sheep, pursuing the slow, personal process of winning individuals by a life of love and holiness, or would he commit himself from henceforth to a program, to the immense grinding of wheels which is a *movement*, and would require more of the things he really disliked: travel, responsibility, promotion, publicity, people? Once he had decided that the movement was the thing, had accepted that basic premise as the work of God for him, then there could be no question that he must go on, seeking ways to "mobilize the membership." There needed to be a redeployment of resources, an alteration in technique, new administrative mechanisms, a vast network of new contacts, new workers, new generators, as it were, to correct a deficiency in power.

It was in defining exactly what was meant by "mobilization" that

Ken encountered the most serious difficulties. He was aware, on the one hand, that in the Body of Christ, that is, among true believers who constitute the Church Universal, there is a variety of gifts and callings. "Not all are called to be prophets or evangelists, there are also the simple gifts of ministering, of mercy, the many unsung and often unrecognized helps that are so essential to the health and testimony of the Body as a whole," Ken wrote in his General Director's message for 1959. Yet it was "personal witnessing"—the very thing for which Ken himself felt poorly qualified—that he believed God demanded of every believer, and it was to this particular aspect of evangelism that he felt every member must be mobilized. "Our entire work could be revolutionized, and an impact made upon our community, such as we have never before attained, if we were to major, individually, and collectively, in a way we haven't before, in witnessing, in continuous visitation work, in the sort of personal contacts and friendships which result in reproduction and in the making of disciples." He warned against fanaticism, extreme zeal, frenzied activity, for these things "come too close to the spirit of some mass movements which completely absorbs and dominates the individual and human personality in subjection to the totalitarian pseudo-absolutes of the party. . . . The driving, impelling force is ultimately demonic." He cited the example of the Lord Jesus, in His simple living among people. There was "unhurried movement and calm, purposeful witnessing in the course of ordinary existence in which the stress was on *being*, without ignoring at the same time the necessity of *doing* and *speaking*."

In order to follow Christ's example, Ken suggested that the missionaries of the LAM should seek in the coming year "continuously to break out of the relative isolationism of our individual and organization involvements and spend more time in *being* ordinary people (not foreign missionaries, not paid religious workers) and in *being with* ordinary people to witness for Christ." The mobilization called for, in the case of these missionaries, amounted almost to a kind of demobilization, an emphasis on being rather than acting, and it is to be wondered what the practical results might have been for the existence of the mission as such had the missionaries complied. How was it to be carried out on a mass scale involving thousands of

Christians in Latin America, while at the same time holding fast to
the truth of the "diversities of operations" of which the apostle Paul
wrote? Is it possible for a movement of any kind, however high its
aim, to avoid dehumanization, diminution of the individual, unifi-
cation? Would it be possible for Ken himself to practice what he
preached to his fellow missionaries, to spend more time being an
ordinary person, being with ordinary people? Would he be able, once
committed to this movement, to be a shepherd to the flock, or would
he be forced to become an operator of machinery? These questions
needled his conscience, for the answers could not be simple. Again
and again he had to silence them by asking the questions that had
simple answers: Was the job being done adequately? Was there
another way to do it? Could he refuse to participate, now that he had
seen the vision? Dare he take any other course? To all of these
questions Ken answered No, a thousand times no.

It was during this year of reflection and re-evaluation that Ken
sent to his children a story about Abraham Lincoln's signing of the
Emancipation Proclamation.

"He had been shaking hands all morning and when the Secretary
of State brought the document to be signed, his hand trembled. He
said, 'If my name ever goes into history it will be for this act, and my
whole soul is in it. If my hand trembles when I sign the Proclamation all who examine the document hereafter will say, "He hesi-
tated." ' Then he turned and picked up the pen and wrote slowly
with a steady hand, 'A. Lincoln.' " Ken added this comment for his
children: "It's not always easy to know the rights of a matter and
there are many areas in life which are not all black and white, rather
grays of differing shades. But where a matter is right then there is
only one thing to do, and that is endorse it by your signature with a
steady hand."

By the end of that year the little dream house in Escazú was
empty again. There had been a blasting radio next door, the house
was too far away from the city, it required more care than the
Strachans could give it—these were some of the reasons for moving.
There were other reasons, which did not seem clear to Ken himself.
He was restless. He felt he ought to be back in the city. The wide-
open spaces, the chickens, the flowering trees and the great solitude

which had held such appeal for him in times when he was denied them, were not, after all, for him. To Elizabeth went the job of trying to find someone to rent the house, for Ken was not yet quite prepared to relinquish it altogether, and he was out of the country again on a speaking tour.

CHAPTER 13

Evangelism-in-Depth was tried out for the first time in Nicaragua, six different cities holding simultaneous campaigns in March, 1960. Ken was in Rivas, a little town where thirty-two years before his father had preached to a small crowd after walking twenty-one kilometers. This time the Gospel message was borne in a much more arresting spectacle—a parade, with banners and flags, cars and horses, bands and marchers. It was watched with scorn, puzzlement, or awe by the citizens of the town. Soldiers and policemen watched, too. There was loud singing—"Onward Christian Soldiers," and "Nicaragua Shall Belong to Christ," sometimes in unison, sometimes with the head of the parade lustily raising one song while the tail carried the other.

"I felt a thrill of pride," Ken wrote, "to be walking beside those Nicaraguan Christians in their brave and dignified witness for Christ." If there had been nothing but sheer volume of activity—the arrangements for hospitality, transportation, literature, meeting places, publicity, music, door-to-door visiting, organization of the parade and the meetings themselves—it would have been impressive. But Ken was able to believe, on this opening night, that he had perhaps found the key which might enable the Church of Christ to meet the challenge of the exploding populations of the world, to "*finish* the job of evangelization."

The meetings continued through March and into April. Ken went to the States to tell of the things that were happening, and in the midst of great eagerness to hear his story he found himself torn by the old misgivings as to just what *he* was doing so deeply involved in this kind of work. "I've been faced with the tremendously competitive brand of life here in the States and the accompanying necessity of self-promotion which prizes and rewards the abilities of self-assurance, the art of making small talk dramatic and important, and the ability to sell oneself, in the face of which I always find myself pulling into my shell and having a fight with all sorts of feelings of inferiority. Had quite a fight with it at———for the first twenty-four hours, but eventually won and came out somewhat at peace with myself and somewhat resigned to being what I am, consoled by the thought that I could be much worse off, and that at least I have you and the children."

The painful question, What am *I* doing here? occurs to very many people at some time in their lives. It requires only a personal answer, as Ken decided in this case. Another emphasis, What am I doing *here?* raises the prior question as to whether the system itself is valid. Has it any serious flaw? If it is accepted as the work of God and one's place in it as the call of God, it is not possible to lay the blame anywhere but on oneself and his own inadequacies. The promise "My sheep hear my voice and they know it" did not cause Ken Strachan to ask whether his own discomfort and uncertainty were the result of listening to a voice that was not that of the Shepherd. Might the pressures that bore him down and the methods he found so tyrannical be of human origin? If, in moments of darkness or weakness, the answer seemed to Strachan to be Yes, he still could not find it in him to doubt that this was the way God was getting His work done in the twentieth century, and he must therefore deny himself and take up his cross and follow.

He visited his three older children who were in boarding school and found Harry "simply a charming boy, thoughtful, intelligent, excellent conversationalist, and unassuming. Cathie is rounded out a bit, much more poised and happy. My heart went out to Robin in a new way. Seemed small and quiet, and I saw in him the little boy that I had been."

He wrote a special letter to Robin on his sixteenth birthday in May. "I can hardly believe that my son Robert is practically entering into manhood. . . . It is strange how we get named. I can't help feeling that the Lord was in it when we named you after me, because

Guatemala campaign of Evangelism-in-Depth, 1962

Strachan (*right*), general director of the Latin America Mission, with his associate Horace L. Fenton on his right, and two assistant general directors, W. Dayton Roberts and David M. Howard

With Billy Graham on the Caribbean crusade tour, 1958

in so many ways I see myself in you and I wonder if you have the same inner fights and fears that I had when I was your age. . . . I wish there were some way of making you realize how very much your mother and dad love you, son. Ever since you came to us you've brought nothing but joy and gladness to our hearts.

"It might be very easy for you to think (specially if you are built at all like your Dad) that our love for you depends on your doing well at school. Just remember, son, that love doesn't lay down conditions, nor limits, nor times. So I hope you'll always count on our love. . . .

"Then another helpful thing is not to think too highly of yourself as the Bible tells us, but at the same time not to sell yourself too cheaply. People will pretty much evaluate you at your own worth. So just because you are smaller physically than some of the others don't give them the idea that you don't think that you're every bit as good. *Hay que hacerse respetar* [You must make yourself respected], as we say in Spanish. And when we are small and somewhat modest (??) as you and I inherently are, it's sometimes hard to learn how to make ourselves respected without becoming stuffed shirts, but our future happiness and success is tied up in it."

In Harry, Ken would tolerate nothing but near perfection, and once wrote, "It is just sheer carelessness to mispell words. . . . Practice each one twenty or more times. No educated person can afford to mispell words." Harry made a list of three words besides *misspell* which his father had misspelled.

When Strachan returned to the campaign in Managua in May he concluded that it had, after all, been "an overwhelming, smashing success." Afterward came the doubts. The Latin American who had been the speaker had perhaps been too polemic. The invitations to accept Christ which were given at the end of the services were very long drawn-out and emotional and had alienated some. Of those who responded to these invitations, it was discovered through later investigation that at least 80 per cent had been superficial and short-lived. Preparation for the campaign had been going on for a year previous, and national pastors felt they had been pushed too hard and too long and could not be expected to pursue a very intensive follow-up of the converts afterward. There was great discouragement among the members of an organization which had promised especially to help in follow-up, and Ken himself wrote that the months after the Nicaragua experiment were his most discouraging. What was wrong? He turned the question over and over in his mind. In a notebook he had copied the following quotation from Pierson's book, *The Divine Enterprise of Missions:* "Christian missions originated with God. The Commission of the Church is from heaven, and can be wrought out only as it was thought out, along the lines and within limits drawn by a hand divine. Here there is no room for human invention or innovation: all such is interference and interruption of the plan of God. All human accretions forming about the pure thought and plan of God—like fungus growths and parasitic mosses about a tree, that both obscure its growth and endanger its life—need to be torn away that we may look again upon the plan of God in its bare simplicity."

Ken wrestled with Pierson's concept. It struck him as a clear, Scriptural statement of the plan of God for a lost world. Evangelism-in-Depth had to fit into this concept somewhere. It had been acclaimed by many mission leaders as a "revolution in ecclesiology," in that evangelism was conceived to be the responsibility of all believers, laity as well as clergy. A revolution implies the overthrow of the former system. If this was a revolution, then the former system must have been a purely traditional one rather than a Scriptural one, for in New Testament churches all believers were "priests," all were "witnesses." Ken had carefully studied the methods of three enormously successful systems—Jehovah's Witnesses, Pentecostalism, and Communism. It was in these that he found his principle of "Total mobilization" which was considered revolutionary, and he regarded his "new" method as in fact a return to the original plan of God. What, then, could be called new about it? Did it differ at all from the simplest forms of witnessing practiced by the first-century Christians? It was a *movement,* indeed. It was highly organized, it had a name, it had an efficient management and a carefully projected program. Was there anything here contradictory to Pierson's statement? Anything that could not be classified as "along the lines and within the limits drawn by a hand divine"? Any human inventions or accretions or innovations? Strachan found nothing. His deep and abiding concern was to see it implemented, and men and money were the two major factors lacking. Men were being supplied. Several capable Latin American men had joined the group and were already participating effectively in the program. Others who were promising had been found. At one point money seemed to be the single factor on which the success of Evangelism-in-Depth depended. Strachan faced the home council with this. "As for Evangelism-in-Depth and its future, let me make you a proposition. Furnish me with $100,000 a year apart from and without detraction from other mission income for the next fifteen years and with God's help, if Christ tarries and He gives me life and health, I'll turn Latin America upside down and carry out an evangelistic movement which will transform and revitalize the evangelical church and its witness in every country, produce a new crop of Latin American leaders, make an impact upon the conscience of Latin Americans, develop a lay movement—such as has never happened in the history of Latin America or of any other part of the world."

It was a staggering claim. But lest the figure of $100,000 should seem to the councilmen exorbitant, Ken pointed out that Billy Graham's annual budget was two and a half million dollars, and Bob Pierce's (of World Vision, Inc.) three million. Strachan proposed to do what had never been done in history with less than a twentieth of the money necessary for others to do what they were doing. "God helping me" is the only uncertain condition except Strachan's own life and health, but his certainty of its being met is evidenced by the confidence with which he went on to outline his plan: "If you were to take me up on such an offer, I would propose that all general administrative responsibilities be carried by Dit, Dayton, and Dave [Howard, director of the Colombia field of the LAM] and I would see to it that they were adequately assisted in the discharge of their duties.

"I would build up an adequate full-time Evangelism-in-Depth staff and immediately set up a program of national movements with four teams, . . . a long-range teaching ministry, pastor's institutes, retreats, Keswicks, rallies, campaigns, literature, and radio ministries, etc.

"I would launch and develop a continental lay movement of business and professional men. . . .

"I would take advantage of every special and auxiliary organization . . . to work out joint efforts mutually advantageous to the extension of our respective ministries and to a greater contribution to the evangelical cause at large.

"What such an expanded program will mean is hard to say—personally I feel it would represent tremendous blessing and boost to every phase and ministry of the LAM."

Did Strachan see clearly what he was doing? Did he see clearly the implications of what he was saying? Did the built-in paradoxes disturb him not at all?

The Strachan circular letter for February, 1961, written by Elizabeth, contains this paragraph:

"It seems that so many of us suffer from at least partial blindness —blindness to all we could be enjoying of the Lord's presence and kindness and also blindness as to the needs and opportunities that surround us. Do we let busyness, activities, and material things crowd out that for which we were made—to know and love God? Do the opinions of other people make us forget that it is going to be before God Himself that we must someday give our account? . . . Or could it be said of us, 'Eyes have they, but they see not'?"

No man sees the whole truth at once. All have "eyes and see not" in some area, and there were things Ken did not see until two years later, when, from a public platform, he confessed that he had been "in a ratrace in Evangelism-in-Depth," that he had found himself posing as an authority where he was no authority. The burden was too heavy to be borne. Such burdens are not those laid on men by Him who said, "My yoke is easy and my burden is light," but must be those laid down by others, or by ourselves—perhaps the burdens Ken himself later called "pseudo-absolutes."

Something snapped. "I was in Colombia," Ken told his audience, referring to a pastors' conference in April, 1961. "I arrived one day, and the next day I was broken in spirit and in health."

Strange things began to happen. In the home where he was a guest his hostess asked whether he would have tea, coffee, or Coca-Cola. He could not decide. When someone else said, "Tea," Ken said he would have tea. When the next person asked for coffee Ken changed his mind. Then, appearing genuinely upset by his perplexity he spoke sharply to the hostess. All those present knew him well, and were stupefied by this wholly uncharacteristic behavior. He began to suffer from intolerable backache. In the meetings while he was speaking he found himself suddenly so weak he had to take hold of the lectern to keep from collapsing. His mind went blank. Sentences wandered on and on without coming to the point. Old illustrations and ideas were resurrected from dusty corners of his mind and presented so dustily that his colleagues looked at one another in consternation. He became dizzy and had terrible headaches.

Various possible ills—mononucleosis or hepatitis, which often strike missionaries—were suggested, but it became alarmingly clear that Ken needed expert help. He was flown to the United States and examined by physicians. The diagnosis: nothing was organically wrong. He was suffering from tension. Some months later he described in a letter what had happened: "I had had a premonition that I had fifteen years to live and I must put my house in order (Isaiah 38:1). But then I experienced a physical breakdown and was knocked out completely for the next five months. Mentally and spiritually I hit bottom or pretty near. In repeated dreams I saw myself dead or felt I was completely washed out as far as the future was concerned."

One of the dreams referred to showed Elizabeth driving the car with the six children in it. Ken was disturbed by the way she was driving and tried to correct it. She paid no attention and he finally realized she could not hear him because he was dead.

Only a month after Ken had flown home from Colombia he was well enough to remember Mother's Day, and sent Elizabeth a bouquet with this message, "I never could, even with red roses, tell you adequately what a wonderful sweetheart, wife, and mother you've been." The note was signed "Sincerely, Ken"—a joking reference to the timid inscription with the first red roses he had sent her during the days of what he now called his "boneheaded courtship."

Once more the time for the annual meetings in New Jersey had come. Ken was not yet well. He had spent the summer in Wheaton, playing golf in the mornings as ordered by the doctors, trying to write in the afternoons, but unable to produce anything that was not stodgy. His legs ached continually and he suffered from headaches and other discomforts. He was not a man to hide his feelings easily if he was uncomfortable, and he dreaded attending the mission meetings where he would be expected to behave as though all were well at least spiritually if not physically. He knew that all was not well in either realm, but he went, sometimes skipping a meeting, sometimes sitting on the back row instead of in his accustomed place on the platform. To add to his personal problems, the mission was in a period of slump. There was a serious financial deficit and the illness of its general director had had a depressing effect on the workers.

Many of the LAM "family" were finding the meetings at Keswick encouraging, and, in answer to prayer, were confident that God would provide. Ken had found no such encouragement. One afternoon he sat on his bed in utter dejection, sure that whatever it was God was doing for the others, He was not doing for him, and he might as well submit his resignation. Jacob Stam, a close friend of many years' standing, and president of the Board of Trustees of the mission, came into the room and began to talk to him. Ken grabbed for a magazine that lay beside him on the bed, then reached instead for his Bible. Something in Stam's words, something which Ken later understood to be the very Spirit of God Himself in his friend, reached his heart, and he was able to return to the mission meetings with hope.

The principal task which they had met to consider, beyond the usual business, would have been overwhelming enough without the handicaps they suffered. Evangelism-in-Depth was about to invade Guatemala.

"Four million Guatemalans to be reached in cooperation with the existing evangelical forces in the course of a single year! Humanly speaking an impossible task—so impossible that one's own body and soul faltered when faced with the decision, rendering him incapable of moving forward," Ken wrote some months later. "In the light of staggering deficits in the preceding months, it was a hopeless proposition. . . . Suddenly we were brought out of the distress of mind to the perfect haven of assurance that God would provide."

It might be expected that nothing but a divine manifestation—a voice, a wind, a fire—could possibly suffice to impart the faith for such a task. The unexplained illness of the director, the financial emergency, the paucity of workers were great needs, but they paled before the spiritual demands implied by the evangelization of four million souls. Who was sufficient for this? The sign which to Ken was the voice of God was not thunder, not a rushing wind or a handwriting on the wall, nor yet even a written promise from Scripture. It was a written promise of five thousand dollars from his friend Stam.

"From such pledges of faith and sacrificial gifts of love in moments of need throughout the long year were God's wondrous works and wonders in the deep made manifest," Ken wrote. And his own sufferings seemed to be over, for a time at least. "It was like coming out of a long tunnel into daylight."

To the LAM family: "Better than ever before I can enter into the experience of mental anguish and spiritual desolation which is repeatedly expressed by God's servants of old in such words as these, 'All Thy waves and Thy billows passed over me. . . . I am cast out of Thy sight.' But I am also entering into their experience of release and joy, of restored faith and renewed strength which invariably followed as God with His perfect timing did His perfect work and which also expressed itself in such words as these, 'This poor man cried and the Lord heard him, and saved him out of all his troubles. O taste and see that the Lord is good: blessed is the man that trusteth in Him.'

"Whatever the physical and spiritual causes, I have the conviction that the experiences of the past months represented a real onslaught of Satan, to hinder the work which the Lord has committed to us in the LAM and to paralyze the movement of Evangelism-in-Depth. . . . Encouraging is the fact that the Enemy should single us out for attack, but much more so the abundant tokens of the Lord's faithfulness and goodness."

Following the Keswick conference Ken went to Mayo Clinic and was thoroughly examined and discharged with no medical findings other than fatigue and tension. He began to worry a little about whether his troubles were "all in the mind," and even felt that to follow the doctors' orders for a drastically reduced schedule of work was a farce. Others persuaded him to follow them, however, so he wrote out some rules for himself:

"1) Reduced schedule of public speaking.

"2) Lay low on type of meetings, conferences, book reviews and article assignments that contribute merely or mostly to personal stature.

"3) Daily Bible study, prayer, waiting on the Lord.

"4) No decisions or commitments without waiting on the Lord.

"5) Regular exercise, rest, relaxation, proper diet.

"6) Cut out travel as much as possible, delegate to others.

"7) Discipline in reading, recreation, work, spending money.

"8) Cultivate greater disinterested interest in other people, praying for them, verbal and written words of encouragement, service."

Among the written words of encouragement were more letters to his children than he had found time for before. His son Harry was in college then, and had written to tell his father of certain doubts as to the validity of the Christian faith, and of a general apathy and depression that had afflicted him. Coming from a man who had so recently emerged from a slough of despond Ken's reply is especially worthy of note:

"It's easy to get into a habit of recurring despondency, self-doubting and self-loathing. What right does a man in good health, with full use of his faculties, who can get out and run (RUN—do you realize what it means to be able to run at full speed?), who gets three square meals a day, who has been endowed with gifts, personality, talents, a better-than-average background and fund of experience and travel, who can believe and say what he believes without hindrance . . . who in addition to all the material and physical blessings of his life has also the indescribable, measureless gift of God's grace —the forgiveness of sins, the restoration to Divine favor, the faithful working of His Spirit, the Chart and Compass of the Word of God, . . . what right does such a man have to talk about wanting to be released from living, from feeling, believing, to talk about ennui and tiredness of life?

"You see, son, it's hard to feel sorry for you, because your troubles aren't real, they're just fancied or imaginary. . . . You're just kidding yourself. . . . I think we need to discern between that fictitious, subjective, self-centered area of feeling and the real world of struggle, temptation, attack, and testing. The Lord knows there's plenty of the latter. Why succumb to the former and thus play into the hands of the Enemy? My experiences of the past months have helped me to see this more clearly and to realize the need for such discernment in my own life."

Harry let this letter "settle" for several hours. It had seemed at first unjust, and as though his father had a "log in his own eye," but then he decided that perhaps he had not missed the mark so widely after all. Harry's mention of doubts about Christianity was largely ignored, and Harry saw that, to his father, "the big thing was to not even in your mind entertain thoughts of dropping out of the game of life or quitting. . . . There were certain areas or subjects of life that at given times he blocked off," Harry wrote later. "Death wishes like headaches were something we all entered into a nonverbal agreement to ignore and in that manner never encourage directly."

The year 1961 ended with Ken in the hospital, this time more ill than he had ever been.

CHAPTER 14

The year 1962 was to be the year of the Evangelism-in-Depth campaign in Guatemala—if there was to be a campaign. After the difficulties encountered in Nicaragua it remained to be seen whether Guatemalan pastors would want to make the experiment in their own country. Ken lay in his hospital bed and thought about it. Had lessons been sufficiently learned in Nicaragua? Would the mistakes that had been made there be repeated, or would they profit by them? Was it reasonable to hope for complete cooperation in a country where Ken himself had seen evidence for years of extreme difficulties and conflicts among Christians? If Evangelism-in-Depth would work in Guatemala, it would probably work anywhere in Latin America. Guatemala would be the supreme test.

In one of Ken's letters to Elizabeth during their courtship he had told her how he loved teamwork. He loved working with other men, and he would love teaming up with her for life. He wanted, naturally, to be free to choose those with whom he was to team, and there was in him also the desire to shut himself away. "I'm terribly selfish and love my own comforts and haven't a great interest in other people's problems and much less patience to listen to them. Probably my tendency will be to shut myself more and more away from many broad contacts. But you mustn't let me do that," he had written in 1940. Elizabeth's efforts had been largely directed toward encouraging her husband to spend time with ordinary people. There was little need for her to push him into "many contacts." He had those. His life had been spent in meetings, interviews, travels, councils, and conferences. He was exhilarated by the new opportunities which Evangelism-in-Depth afforded for moving out of the old line. He was seeing one of his fondest dreams come true, that of working side by side with Latin Americans like Rubén Lores from Cuba who had been a missionary in North Africa and a pastor in New York and who brought to the team creative and penetrating insights into missionary strategy and principles; Juan Isais from Mexico whom as a young man Ken had introduced to evangelistic work. Ken was to Juan as the apostle Paul to young Timothy, an older brother in the Lord, encouraging and directing him. Jonás Gonzalez, also of Mexican background, was another Timothy to Ken. He had graduated from the seminary in San José and had been a Baptist minister in Dallas, Texas, before joining the Evangelism-in-Depth team at Ken's invitation.

The Partnership Program initiated years before had aimed at the kind of teamwork which Evangelism-in-Depth was actually accomplishing. Besides the Latins with whom Ken worked there were missionaries of many differing views and backgrounds whom Ken succeeded in drawing together into a common group with a supreme objective. They saw his determination not to be bound by every shackle that bound them and although this caused criticism from some quarters, the majority learned to appreciate his openness and liberty. He gained recognition in circles where he had been unknown before. He reveled in the intimate teamwork which he had enjoyed for years with his close colleagues, Dit Fenton, Dayton Roberts, and Dave Howard. They were men of widely differing moods and temperaments who met frequently for planning and direction of the mission. Sparks sometimes flew. Ken could disagree hotly and find himself pounding the table. Dit interspersed business with humor, occasionally teasing Ken almost beyond mercy. He and Dave were regarded by the other two as too cautious at times, lacking in daring and vision. But all believed in the Scriptural secret of harmony, "in honor preferring one another."

In meetings of the executive committee he would often be carried away by enthusiasm for the particular project he had been working on, and it was difficult to persuade him to give equal attention to the projects or problems of the others. If he had just come from the

States his mind was filled with deputation, promotion, or ideas he had picked up on his travels, while if he had been in Colombia he could hardly concentrate on the Costa Rica side of the work. If his faith was prepared to embrace some new expansion or development it was with the greatest difficulty that the other team members made him see that such a move would mean overextension or financial imbalance.

Ken believed very strongly that the will of God for members of the mission must be determined by joint consultation and consent. If any man or woman had been led to join the mission, then it followed that they ought to be prepared for decisions arrived at "in the multitude of counsellors." Once, however, Ken himself was at odds with the home council, and this presented an altogether different situation. He wrote to Elizabeth that he earnestly hoped that they would see things his way, but that if not, he would simply have to pray about it and "then make my own decision, and hope they will concur."

It was partly Ken's consciousness of his own Irish propensity to moodiness and emotional reaction that made him want a team administration. He prided himself on the democracy of the organization, and the majority of the missionaries would have agreed that there was a great freedom and mutual trust within the organization. Some, however, felt they were but "pawns" and regretted Ken's seeming inability to relate to "ordinary" people. He was drawn to wealthy people, famous people, people of station in life, and he could be his warmest and kindest with humble people or sick people. It was striking to note, after his death, how many of these two classes considered Ken Strachan their very closest friend. But he himself was the first to acknowledge his diffidence with strangers. He seldom distributed religious tracts, an activity often taken for granted among missionaries as a necessary part of their work. He once said that his work had been limited to mass evangelism and he simply did not know how to talk of Christ to an individual. Although he would sometimes get up from a sickbed when told that some simple peasant was there to see him, he would often ask Elizabeth to shield him from the intrusions of his peers.

*

It must have been hard for Ken himself to know what he really wanted as he lay in the hospital. Memories of defeats in Nicaragua must have tormented him. Would Guatemala be like that? If so, wouldn't it be better not even to try a campaign? If he were sick enough perhaps it would be postponed. "O ye of little faith!" The words of the Lord must have come to him. If he, the leader of the movement, had no more faith than that, how could he expect others to exercise it? No, he must get well. He must go to Guatemala. But then, he did not even know with certainty whether the pastors wanted a campaign. But surely they would. Surely they had not been led thus far for nothing. The men of faith in the Bible were men who did not quit. He could not quit merely because of the unhappy elements in the Nicaragua experience. It was probably meant to test his faith. He used to tell his children that "a big shot is a little shot who never stopped shooting." This was no time to stop.

Unknown to Ken, many pastors in Guatemala had agreed to pray for his healing. Some of them were meeting at five o'clock in the morning for this.

They got exactly what they asked for. Within a few weeks Ken was on his way to Guatemala, this time with Elizabeth, because the doctor had ordered him not to travel alone. Two thousand pastors had gathered for a conference. Arriving while one of the meetings was in session the Strachans tried to slip into a back row. Someone let it be known that Kenneth Strachan had come, and the two thousand rose together in ovation. For a man who knew that "man looketh on the outward appearance but God looketh on the heart," and had no confidence in either the one aspect or the other, for a man who had once declared himself "doomed to mediocrity," it was a stunning tribute.

The pastors had decided that they wanted Evangelism-in-Depth in Guatemala. It seemed to them the only answer to their need, and they were prepared to sacrifice, to work, to cooperate. It was the cooperation that would cost them more than they had realized, and Ken stood up before them and clearly explained what they would have to do. Each group had its own plans to consider, each pastor his own program. All these would have to take second place. There was no other way, and although argument ensued and Latin tempers flared, Ken quietly and stubbornly insisted that this was basic to the success of the venture. He explained, too, the financial responsibility that would rest with the Guatemalans themselves. He carefully outlined the rationale of the movement and its methods of preparation and follow-up, ending with a forceful sermon in which he attacked their lack of faith and their cheapness with God's work. None dared to raise any objection to this, and at last the pastors consented to support the campaigns as Strachan said they must be supported. His utter assurance that he was right and that he had been guided by God Himself in the conception of his plan was supported by other evangelical leaders. Arthur Glasser of the Overseas Missionary Fellowship said, "In present missionary thinking, I see nothing comparable with its vision and dynamic. . . . This marks a heartening breakthrough in the sinful tangle of inertia that has delayed for so long the advance of the Gospel both at home and overseas. Thank God."

When it came time for the election of an executive committee for the Guatemala campaign, gears began to grind because of disagreements. Ken was called upon to conduct the nominating. Apparently reluctant at first, he took charge, and after a speech in which he tried to impress upon the members the seriousness of the tasks ahead of each officer, he opened the floor for nominations. When he decided there were enough he himself closed them. When someone wanted to introduce another candidate he did not permit it. In a similar manner a vice president was elected. Only one member was reported to have been dissatisfied with the proceedings.

In February Ken wrote, "Inclined to believe that the Lord's pattern for me may be to settle down in some center and concentrate on master-minding the development of Evangelism-in-Depth and other ministries in Latin America. It may be necessary for me to adopt a hard and fast rule of practically cutting out all travel. But can I?"

The answer to that question appears to have been negative. Before the year was over he had traveled to Guatemala, Costa Rica, the United States, Guatemala again, Colombia, Guatemala, Costa Rica, Colombia, Panama, Colombia, Ecuador, and back again to Guatemala. His long-suffering wife wrote in one of the family circulars of that year, "It is always dangerous to announce future movements, but as of the moment the family plans to remain here until June. . . . In my weaker moments, I long almost passionately for a more settled existence. . . ."

Somehow Ken managed to find time to write a twenty-two-page memo covering the next ten years' program for evangelism. "If the Lord were to take me now I would at least have left a 'testament' of conviction re: the mission of the Mission," he wrote. In an article for the *Evangelist* entitled "Discipleship Must Cost" he referred to the communistic manner of life of the early Christians who "had all things in common," and raised the question whether Christians are not being called upon in this day to sacrifice earthly goods for the sake of needy brethren. During a visit to Guatemala he had observed the way of life of one of the national pastors. "As I took in the physical conditions, the heat and discomfort, . . . the gnawing frustration of economic pressure, something inside of me kept crying out, 'It isn't fair!' This is something which we as a mission must grapple with officially."

Strachan was a man of vision, a man capable of seeing things afar off and working out ways and means (often "official" ones) of grappling with a thousand varieties of problems which he saw to be related to the spiritual need of the world, and at the same time inexplicably blind to needs much closer home, entirely "unofficial" needs. Was the material privation of the Guatemala pastor greater or more unfair than the emotional privation of his own family? Elizabeth had tacitly accepted for years his long absences from home, struggling always to concede that they were "necessary," as Ken insisted. But at last she began to feel that they might be really wrong, that there were reasons other than her own loneliness and Ken's health for curtailing his travels, and she wrote to him about this.

"Dearest Ken, which would you rather have—no letter at all or a sad one? I can't explain it, but in a way difficult to describe, I'm simply and completely fed up with being a widow and having a traveling husband. I won't go into details but last night I dreamed you had come home, was simply ecstatic, when just as you bent down to kiss me you vanished again, and I woke up with the emptiest of feelings. And just the thought of keeping on writing these endless letters leaves me absolutely ill. Twenty-two years of letters *ya basta* [is plenty]. . . .

"Darling, I love you, and I realize it is hopeless and useless to suggest it, but I'm sure you could have a fruitful, less strenuous, more economical ministry stationed right here in San José than wearing yourself out jumping from one place to another. Evangelism-in-Depth hasn't scratched the surface in San José. The believers here are not engaged in a continuous movement of evangelism. I'm trying to get my class to give one afternoon a week to visitation, but even that will only be a drop in the bucket. I think if you'd get Costa Rican believers really united in evangelism, it would be a wonderful example to the rest of the continent—maybe wouldn't make as big a splash, but might be a more solid piece of work. Think and pray about it.

"Sometimes I get the awful feeling you will never be coming back. I don't know why, but this stretch has seemed almost endless.

"Just know that I love you with all the love I'm capable of, and we three here are just longing for you to come home."

In another letter she said, "If I were to send you a recording, I think I'd send the hymn, 'Come home, come home, ye who are weary, come home.' " Then she added in pencil in the margin. "O sinner, come home!"

One of Ken's children said, "My father was a very complicated man." In this he did not differ from most men, nor did he differ in his inability to see himself accurately. That he could have lived the kind of life he lived and written at the same time the following, is one of the paradoxes that must be faced and accepted, if not explained. It was in an editorial which bore the title, "The Tyranny of the Pseudo-Absolutes," that he described an Indian toiling up a mountain road bent down under an enormous stack of homemade pottery. The missionary watches him and wonders why he makes himself a beast of burden.

"That missionary who passes the Indian on the mountain road—who is he working for? What makes him run so? True, he is driving a car and carries no physical load on his back. But is he a free man or also a slave? For it is possible that he too may be living in bondage—to burdens imposed by the past, by tradition, by society, by his fathers. Or is it possible that he may be living in slavehood under a tyranny of his own making?

"How this can happen to a Christian who has been set free by the Son is passing strange. But it happens . . . and to a greater degree than one likes to admit. Our frequent failure to distinguish between truth and half-truths (not to speak of error) makes us the repeated dupes of faulty premises, wrong conclusions, and deceptive rationalizations. We forge unscriptural and unnecessary shackles, we set up artificial priorities and imperatives and the end result brings us under the tyranny of unwarranted pseudo-absolutes. . . .

"The problem for us is that—like the Indian—we hardly recognize the nature of our bondage. Those regulations, those goals, that schedule, those driving forces, those lords of our lives which demand our energies and activities, which exact the last ounce of strength in endless servitude, can they possibly be pseudo-absolutes? Have we not always prided ourselves, on our rectitude and consecration to these imperatives and identified them with the will and work of God? How could anyone possibly confuse them with the false gods that others serve? . . .

"How easy and unconscious, for example, the process by which a rightful loyalty to one's own denomination, or a natural concern for the growth of one's local church, or a worthy zeal for one's own organization can be transformed into motivations that are essentially egocentric and potentially demonic. How easy it is to set up human traditions and regulations in place of the Word of God, to mistake human interpretations for the Word itself and thus come into bondage.

"The tragedy is that the slave of the pseudo-absolutes can never deliver another from bondage. He can only add to his burdens, or exchange them for others; he can only extend the tyranny of his false lord. His efforts are doomed. A judgment has been passed upon them. 'You bind heavy burdens on men's shoulders. . . . You compass sea and land to make one proselyte, and make him two-fold more the child of hell than yourselves. Woe to you!' "

While Ken was on a plane to Guatemala in November he read a book which caused him to begin praying for the third time for a baptism of the Holy Spirit. In his notebook he wrote, "Went forward in the Olympic Gymnasium that night to seek God's blessing, and have been rising each night for Bible reading and prayer since then. I don't know 'what to ask for as I should'—whether *the* baptism of the Spirit or a fresh anointing—but I am asking God to give whatever I need of the Holy Spirit including such gifts—tongues, healing, prophecy, etc.—as He wills. And in presenting this petition to the Lord I am aware that in me I can in no way fulfill the essential persistency, perseverance, utter committal and faith to obtain. So on the basis of Luke 11:13 I hope and come." The verse cited says, "If you, then, who are evil, know how to give good gifts to your children, how much more will the heavenly Father give the Holy Spirit to those who ask Him?"

There is no record of an answer to this prayer, but his prayers for Guatemala could not, in his eyes, have been more fully granted. He wrote to his children in December, 1962:

"I wish that you could have been with me last week. Fantastic is the only word to describe it. Our capital city crusade had been a rather difficult affair with more than the ordinary share of problems to overcome, so that I personally wasn't very optimistic when I left San José to go up for the last days and in order to meet our party of thirty North American friends of Operation Outreach. But we couldn't have put on a better show if we had engineered it ourselves. Friday night—a banquet in the American Club with the President of the Republic; Saturday night an overflow crowd of at least 12,000 in the Olympic Gymnasium; and then Sunday morning a four-hour revolution during which we watched the Guatemala Airforce in revolt dive-bombing and strafing the Presidential House and other strategic locations in the city while the ground forces countered with anti-aircraft batteries and while we wondered what was going to happen to our parade scheduled for one o'clock and to the final rally scheduled for three in the big stadium.

"To make the story short (because I'm too sleepy), in spite of the revolution and all rumors to the contrary, the parade was rolling by two, and was a tremendous demonstration of Guatemalan valor as a three-mile-long parade of over fifteen thousand evangelicals went through the main streets of the city to the stadium. That afternoon some thirty thousand people sat in the rain and listened to the

Gospel. Wonder of wonders the president of the republic and about forty of his men attended, every single one of them with a machine gun slung over his shoulder. Unshaven and tieless they had been up all night and fighting all morning, and yet there they were for the meeting. They sat in the presidential box right across from where our party was sitting and as you can imagine our folks got a tremendous thrill out of the whole affair. God certainly answered prayer for the entire effort."*

* For a more complete account of this and other campaigns see W. Dayton Roberts, *Revolution in Evangelism* (Chicago: Moody Press, 1967).

CHAPTER 15

Every man goes through life essentially alone, and R. Kenneth Strachan was no exception. In addition to the physical separation from his parents at an early age and from his family for a large percentage of his adult life, there was a feeling of estrangement by temperament from his colleagues in the work—he was never quite free from the uncomfortable suspicion that they somehow "belonged" more than he. His natural reticence and lack of curiosity about people he had fought desperately to overcome, to *be* for others, and in this struggle he was alone within himself. Loved as well as respected by his children, he loved them in return and made a point of writing them special letters on their birthdays, of promising them special privileges as the reward of work they had done to please him. He agonized alone over them, writing out for himself questions about one or another in order to seek the answers: "Is he trying to break away from the little world of Fundamentalism?" "Is he being blind to the real nature of the world he admires? Has he created a synthetic tension in his mind against which he revolts? What's wrong?" He tried to take each child, at some time in his life, somewhere alone with him. His daughter Clare remembers going with him to a Bible conference. "*Kindness* is what I most remember about him. I was very proud of him. He wasn't always a sharp dresser, but I was proud of him. I thought to myself, 'People will like him. I don't have to worry. And even if they don't, he's worth something.' I would walk down the street on his arm."

A relationship existed between Ken and his nephew Paul Roberts that was distinct from the relationship he had with any of his own children. Paul was born with a deformed right hand, and when he was growing up Ken once sent him a poem entitled "To Christopher" (Christopher was Paul's first name) by G. A. Studdert-Kennedy:

> Bear thou the Christ,
> My little son.
> He will not burden thee,
> That Holy One.
> For, by a mystery,
> Who beareth Him He bears
> Eternally,
> Up to the radiant heights
> Where Angels be,
> And heaven's crimson crown of lights
> Flames round the crystal sea.*

He took special pains to teach Paul to bat with his left hand. He sent him Christmas and birthday cards, visited him at boarding school, wrote him letters, and, when Paul was in college and Ken had been having treatments at Mayo Clinic, Ken tried to persuade him to go to the clinic to see if the doctors there might not be able to do something for his hand.

Strachan was never publicly embarrassed by his children's behaving like typical rebellious "preachers' kids." They were decorous in conduct. But he suffered privately over their fundamental doubts about Christianity. Three of the children were in college in 1963 and during vacations there were some ferocious debates on questions which a liberal arts education necessarily raises. With his oldest son Ken was able to give and take in a controlled, reasonable way. Harry knew how to expose himself and analyze his feelings so as to attract rather than frighten or alienate his parents. He had written to his father to describe a dream in which his father was slightly critical of Harry's excellent diving technique. "Thanks for sharing your dream with us, Harry," Ken replied. "Isn't it amazing how poignantly real a dream can be? It moved me deeply too as I read your description and realized how I'm tied to your life like an albatross tied to your neck. And I haven't the slightest idea of how to release

* From *The Unutterable Beauty*, (New York: Harper & Brothers, 1930).

you, except to say that little by little as you gain experience and develop proficiency in your own field or specialty that this sense of dependence will gradually wear away, and you will be freed from me and perhaps at liberty to get acquainted with me. . . . In the meantime I want you to know that it's not so much the voice of your father that is always urging you on but rather that inner driving force to excel that will never allow you to rest and that will be the cause of much of your unrest and unhappinesss for the next few years at least, but will also be God's gift to you to make you into something. And don't let that voice deceive you into thinking that I am critical of you or of your abilities. I would never be able to describe adequately the feelings of pride and satisfaction that I have for you, son. For twenty-one years you have brought nothing but joy and pleasure to us, have made me marvel at your sense of responsibility and maturity, your discipline and ambition, the inner honesty of your thought-life and desire to serve the Lord and your many gifts and talents. You are so far ahead of anything that I ever was that I have nothing but love and admiration for you, and my constant prayer is that somehow you will be kept and that the Lord will deliver you from any fatal mis-step or spiritual tragedy."

The son who was named after him Ken found increasingly difficult to understand. Robert had studied philosophy, sociology, psychology, and biology and challenged his father with questions that had not occurred to him before. Ken became angry, frustrated, baffled. It was one thing to defy God—he himself had done that. It was another to question His existence. This Ken had never done. Not in the nadir of his deepest periods of depression had he ever known what it was to wonder whether God was *there*. He had always been able to insist that He was, and that whatever seemed to be the absence of visible signs of His presence had a purely personal explanation and could be attributed to Ken's own spiritual state. Failures must be blamed on himself, never on God. He was impatient with questions which he had settled long ago. Why should not his sons take his word for it? Robert was not easily pacified by his father's "I-know-I'm-right-you'll-see-it-someday" attitude. Nor could Ken easily dismiss Robert's problems, confident as he might have been that the Lord would some day lay hold of him.

He wrote to Harry asking him to help Robert, "who goes about his job, selling Bibles, door to door, feeling like an orphan in the universe. . . . This tears my heart. He's such a swell kid, so loving and honest, and I hate the thought of his spending any time with the lights out inside." For some reason, Robert's doubts seemed more real to Ken than Harry's had the year before, when he had written, "Your troubles just aren't real," and he wondered this time if he himself could be at fault.

Years before he had written a paper at seminary on "The Reason for Faith." To some of his children this made sense. "I believe in order to understand," was the theme, and for Ken this settled the question. There were areas where mystery remained. There were questions for which there were no answers to be found this side of Eternity. But he had decided that he would "play it for keeps," and there was no use spending one's life tossing the same questions back and forth. John, his youngest son, said, "He helped me—not always toward the right answers, but toward the right attitudes."

Ken could sometimes exhibit a surprising degree of resiliency in meeting the shock of his children's doubts. One of them, in a rare outburst, accused her mother of not having accepted her for what she was, but of trying constantly to make her over into something she was not, and added, "I want you to accept me! If I decide there *is no God*, I still want you to accept me!" Ken's reply was, "Amen!"

He had learned one terribly important lesson at last, after years of torment and self-condemnation: he had come to accept himself, and he saw clearly that he must accept others. He told the children what he had learned, in a letter written to all of them:

"Sooner or later every man has to come to terms with several things in his existence:

"1) with himself. This means accepting himself as he is or as God made him, and in the circumstances in which God placed him . . . be he short or tall, fat or thin, happy-go-lucky or worry-wart, dumb or smart. Only until he does so can he begin to lick the bugaboos of self-pity, inferiority feelings, and inner unhappiness. Even then he's going to have a hard enough time as it is.

"2) He has to come to terms with the world around him, accepting the conditions and laws of life, and giving up the unrealism of a false idealism or the escapism of a dream world.

"3) He has to come to terms with his fellow man, accepting the

laws and obligations of society without however giving up his own
personal liberty. In short, he's got to remain his own man, no matter
what the rest of the world thinks.

"4) He has to come to terms with God. This sounds very easy, to
hear the glib preaching of some people. It sounds impossible, to hear
the sophisticated rationalizations of others. But on some middle
ground of sober thinking and realistic perception one has to make a
choice between God and all the other alternatives. And before one
puts off coming to terms with God he'd better face the alternatives
and satisfy himself that any one of them cannot truly satisfy. I think
that Peter had an intuitive insight into the fact that apart from God
there is no valid explanation of human existence or satisfying relationship for man when he said, 'Lord, to whom shall we go? Thou
hast the words of eternal life.'

"5) He has to accept that his loving parents will abound in exhortations and advice of which all the above constitutes an excellent
example."

His first letter of the year 1963 was written to the children while
Elizabeth was at church one Sunday evening. He told how he had
been displeased with the necktie she had given him for Christmas
and had said, "I'll choose my own ties in the future." While at home
alone he suddenly saw what he had done. "The Lord melted me
down and there swept over me such a realization of Elizabeth's
goodness to me down through the years and all the criticalness and
ungratefulness that she has had to put up with as to make me weep.
So one of my prayers and hopes for this coming year is that the Lord
will give me a grateful heart for all His many blessings, not the least
of which is your mother."

Ken was more aware than many men are of the blessings his wife
had brought him, and expressed his appreciation to her frequently in
his letters. He was not better equipped than most husbands to enter
enter into his wife's interests and problems. He thought she had done
a commendable job in rearing the family. He was only vaguely aware
of what this had cost her, especially on account of his long absences.
He fully expected her to share in his interests and she met his expectations, but when she succeeded in writing three small books* and

* A Mother's Wages, Dear Ann, and True Treasures, all published by Moody
Press, Chicago.

getting them published he simply never got around to reading them, and even misquoted the title of one in a letter to her.

He became increasingly aware of his failings as he grew older, and tried harder than ever to correct them. In order to jog his memory he kept a little black notebook. He found a certain pleasure in making lists and then checking them off. On a trip to Quito, Ecuador, where he spoke to a gathering of three hundred missionaries, he reminded himself to

"1) send regards to———

"2) see that———gets the correspondence course

"3) keep———and———in mind and prayers

"4) write article on———

"5) get———for conference speaker in San José."

There were quotations from books he had been reading (for another resolution was to read more good books)—Martin Luther, John Wesley, T. S. Eliot, Dostoevski, Pasternak. There were pages of notes on planning for future evangelistic projects, with charts, statistics, logistics, organizational changes, publicity ideas, and suggestions to be made to individual team members. There were pages labeled "Ideas" on which he had written things like:

"1) Prayer mat—to map out LAM activity; to be sold in U.S. at summer camps and Bible conferences.

"2) Christian Charm Institute—to practice *witnessing*. Fun, eats, gifts, two chairs in the center of the room, volunteers to practice their 'charm' as though on train or bus, witnessing for Christ.

"3) Plans for reaching:
professional class
labor
political parties
government
business
arts and entertainment

"4) Forum in San José on civic issues, for TV

"5) Slide series on 'The Answer' (to college students' problems)

"6) 'Dorothy Dix' of the Air—advice to the lovelorn

"7) Strategic training center for new missionaries to Latin America

"8) Card questionnaires of
    missionary kids' attitudes to parents
    laymen's toward church."
On one page of the notebook he had written:
"To do:
  1) Get organized
  2) Talk to wife
  3) Get reorganized."
There was, in this year, one final exchange of letters between Elizabeth and Ken on the subject of his traveling.

"I never intend to mention the matter again," Elizabeth wrote. "I think you are making a mistake, partially deceiving your own self, creating needless squirrel cages and travel schedules for both yourself and others, leaving untouched ever so many fruitful doors of service that require no air tickets . . . because of wrong concepts and premises that you have chosen to believe in because of an inner restlessness, lack of discipline in being able or liking to follow routine assignments. . . . You will never willingly stay settled, so any non-travel I might achieve through sanctions of any sort wouldn't be worth working for. You have ever so many wonderful qualities and I plan to meditate on them . . . and to bury once and for all in silence my disapproval and consequent difficulties. Well, dear, keep this vow for me to read should I ever break it."

"There is something to be said on your side, I know," Ken replied, "and perhaps you need to keep saying it in order to force me to give it proper consideration. On the other hand, it makes me feel left alone as far as my calling and mission life, and I wonder if in your process of reasoning you have truly tried to evaluate and give proper credit to such experiences of God's leading and working in my life which have resulted in the call to evangelism and to consequent travel?"

"Ken, I think I'll change my vow to 'I will never bring up the traveling subject unless you bring it up.' . . . I think God does use you on trips, but not any more than He would or could use you, were you able to stick to twelve disciples and build them up and then take twelve more. . . . I think to take a trip now and then to get a new perspective is all to the good, but to make traveling and evangelizing synonymous is all false and wrong—so much wasted energy in movement that could be spent in actual work. . . . Since your one or two innocent observations brought up all those fervid thoughts, I'm sure you'll never mention it again, but anyway I love you, and you have basic weaknesses to put up with in me, things you know are wrong and that will never change, and yet you are so kind and good to me."

Ken's answer to the above was a postscript to the first reply. "Jonás just came in with your letter which is practically your answer to what I've written above. Somewhere beyond us both lies the one real question—what is God's will for us? Let's not write anymore on the subject but be praying. I love you."

Apparently the result of the praying was an assurance on Ken's part that God's will was what it had been all along. He kept on traveling, covering in the remainder of that year the United States, Panama, Paraguay, and Argentina, where he had been invited to participate in a pastors' retreat. It was his first visit back to the land of his birth, and after forty-five years he felt like Rip Van Winkle. He told of sleeping in the house his father had built. "I looked upon the corridor (same old tile) down which as children we'd skipped to lunch, pulling Father with us; wandered in a yard that, though altered, was full of chilhood memories; preached to a packed-out audience in the church that Father built; was tearfully embraced by scores of elderly people, fruit of those early years. . . . As the bus droned through the hours of the night and finally made its way past the endless suburbs of Buenos Aires in the gray light of breaking dawn, so many thoughts floated like jetsam to the surface of consciousness in the jolting half-sleep of the night: 'Your labor is not in vain in the lord.' If I ever wanted any proof of the eternal reward of serving a missionary lifetime in one small village (in their case, eighteen years) I've had it."

Of the pastors' meetings he wrote, "My first message yesterday was typical of all the agony I go through so frequently and also of the way in which the Lord so frequently answers my prayer of desperation. You'll remember, dear, the days of preparation up at the farm. Then as the hour approached, I could feel my stomach churning and the battle with doubt and fear. I took a pill the night before so I'd get some sleep. Got up early and my mind was thick and spirit unresponsive and had to go up on the platform without an outline, my previous thoughts all confused and disordered, and a heavy presentiment of disaster. I sat there, looking at that vast crowd of pastors trying to buck up my courage, and then I was introduced and reading the Scripture passage, and as I did, that spinetingling experience that comes every now and then of knowing that the Lord was with me. What a joy then to speak out, to sense the Lord's working, to see faces glowing or softening in tears, and to feel oneself in that moment to be a spokesman for God and an instrument of blessing. There's nothing like it, but it's only an occasional experience."

Many who sat in Strachan's audiences would have taken issue with the word "occasional." To them, he nearly always had a "word fitly spoken." There was a simplicity about him, an ease and lack of pretension, they said, which drew them. Perhaps the explanation of this lies in an editorial he wrote in 1954:

"I sat looking at the letter in my hand. It contained only two sentences and the words were spread over the entire page in uneven letters blocked out by a little hand. All that it said was, "Dear Daddy: How are you. I love you. Clare.' A whole sheet of paper just to say that!

"But what other words could have expressed more adequately to a missionary on his travels the love and thought of a little daughter? Those poorly drawn lines painted a picture no artist could draw of a little girl with golden hair and blue eyes bent over a piece of paper, pencil in fist, learning to write. . . .

"We cannot speak, we cannot sing, we cannot write except in 'large letters'—awkward, imperfect. We are still children and each has his thorn in the flesh. We still speak and think and understand as children. Some day we shall write with a bold flourish and perfect script.

"But now—if we could only realize the power and purpose and potentiality of our limitations and infirmities! If we could only remember that God has always gloried in choosing the foolish things, the weak things, the base things and the things which are not in order that His power might be revealed to us in our weakness and through us that the glory might be all His.

" 'There is in weakness something that can take possession of our hearts until they ache with tenderness that strength cannot evoke.' "

Evangelism-in-Depth was reaching other countries, and reports had spread widely of its successes. It was to be expected that there would be criticism, not only of the program itself but of the organization which had sponsored it and specifically of its leader. The Latin America Mission found itself suspected of "liberalism" and "inclusivism" and other heresies, of which it had been accused in years past. Strachan had given considerable thought to the basis of cooperation, the *sine qua non* of the movement, and although it cost him some sleepless nights and some literal headaches, he felt that everything must be risked for the sake of bringing together the greatest number of Bible-believing Christians for the greatest possible effort to evangelize. "What if our financial support falls off?" "What if the reputation of the mission is jeopardized?" These and other questions plagued him, and in order to make his position as clear as possible he issued a statement on the Latin America Mission and the Question of Relations and Cooperation.

"Two missionaries are discussing a problem that faces Christians all over the world today. The problem is this: Amid the confusion of professing churches of Christ and the doctrinal variety and confusion, with whom should they fellowship and with whom cooperate?

"One of them says, 'If anyone teaches erroneous doctrine contrary to the Word of God, *I will not* have fellowship with that person. It would be disloyalty to my Lord if I did not separate from him completely.'

"The other one says, 'If anyone really loves the Lord Jesus Christ sincerely and honestly desires to obey Him according to the light he has received, *I must have* fellowship with that person, no matter how deficient some of his beliefs seem to be. I cannot separate myself from my fellow-lover of the Lord as though he were not a member of the body of Christ.' . . .

"Unfortunately the question involves not merely personal relationship but also church and organizational relations as well. . . . Respective attitudes about relating to other professing Christians seem to have become the touchstone by which they may recognize or enjoy fellowship with each other."

The paper includes a history of the LAM and its policy of cooperation since its beginning, a summary of basic convictions, and a conclusion:

"In the discharge of our ministry we will not knowingly link ourselves to anyone who denies our Lord. At the same time, in faithfulness to Scriptural injunction and example, we shall not necessarily cut ourselves off from contacts which might result in the correction of an erring brother or the salvation of some captive soul. . . . We ask for Christian courtesy, and respect for the Scriptual liberty of judgment and conscience in Christ. 'If any man trust to himself that he is Christ's, let him of himself think this again, that, as he is Christ's, even so are we Christ's.' "

When Ken went to Lima, Peru, in January 1964, it was with the hope of securing cooperation among all evangelical groups working there, in order that Evangelism-in-Depth might operate in that country. There had been interest shown, and an invitation to Ken and others to come, but when the group met dissension arose, there was intransigence on the part of some, and although some felt that steps had been taken toward future cooperation, Ken's hopes disintegrated. He did not live to see them realized, but as this book is being written Evangelism-in-Depth is in operation in Peru.

It was while Ken was in Peru that one of his colleagues called his attention to some nodules on his neck. Upon returning to San José in February he saw a doctor, who immediately sent him to New York for further investigation. Knowing that his condition might be serious, he left a note of special appreciation for his secretary, which she later interpreted to mean that he had had a premonition of his death. To others, however, he appeared quite unconcerned, and wrote a circular letter in March telling of the doctors' assurance, by that time, that his disease was not Hodgkin's, as had at first been suspected, and clearing him to go "full steam ahead" with his planned schedule of teaching for four months in California.

"Elizabeth and I came out of his office rejoicing in God's goodness and with a sneaking little suspicion that He had intervened in answer to prayer. . . . 'How excellent is thy lovingkindness, O God! Therefore the children of men put their trust under the shadow of Thy wing.' "

It seemed to Ken that God had arranged things well for the next few months. He was lecturing on missions at Fuller Seminary in Pasadena and the family were living in a comfortable house nearby. There were competent physicians available in case he needed them, and the long-dreamed-of life of quiet study and reflection which had not lasted long at the ranch house in Escazú appeared to be within reach here.

The task of preparing and delivering his lectures presented to Ken the usual difficulties of a sense of unworthiness and a fear that he would not perform as well as required, but if the testimony of men who were there can be taken rather than Ken's own, his fears were unfounded. Few visiting professors are remembered with such unqualified praise. "His combination of awareness in theology, creativity in church strategy, charity in personal relations, and discipleship in heart attitude gave us an object lesson of what it means to find our wholeness in Jesus Christ," wrote the president of the seminary. A student wrote, "You hardly seemed like a professor. You were more like the Apostle Paul and we . . . well, we were like the scared crewmen on the stormy sea. Many of us had given up hope for the missionary enterprise. Evangelism was not an option. All our hopes and ambitions would soon be smashed on the rocks. Many of us despaired of life itself. The wind had torn the sails. We had already thrown the rigging overboard. And we were so tired and hungry. Then you stepped out on the deck. Somehow all of us, from the captain to the sailors, felt you should take charge. When you said, 'I now bid you to take heart; for there will be no loss of life among you, only the ship. . . . So take heart, men, for I have faith in God' we could hardly believe you. 'Why, don't you know the theological climate in this part of the world?' some of the sailors muttered. 'There is no hope; we are all going under.' But because you spoke with such love and hope, reinforced by your life, we believed you.

"You had us over to your house. You asked us who we were and why we were in seminary. You loved us and gave yourself to us."

Ken had an urge to simplify and formulate which found an outlet in the classroom, but he was not easily satisfied with pigeonholes. He was most impatient with anything that seemed to him pompous or superficial. When friends wanted him to see Pasadena's famous Rose Tournament he expressed his disdain of parades—"frivolity," he called it. (The parades formed for introducing an Evangelism-in-Depth campaign he regarded very differently, perhaps because of their serious purpose.) Even Christmas decorations he thought ridiculous.

While in southern California he was introduced to some things which all his life he had looked upon as worldly and therefore worthless or even dangerous. Friends persuaded him and Elizabeth to attend a Spanish drama which included dancing at Padua Hills. He was overcome by the beauty of it all. "We have been defrauded!" was his exclamation afterward. "It is wrong to forbid Christians such things." The implications of this revelation to a man whose activities had been so stringently circumscribed for so long, but whose mind was at times capable of seeing truth regardless of its dress, might have been much more devastating than in fact they were had he been in better health at the time. He was ill and had all he could do to handle his lectures at the seminary.

In May he was taken to the hospital violently ill. A few weeks later he resumed his duties, but throughout the summer symptoms recurred and he was in frequent pain. In September he reluctantly agreed to another series of tests, although he found it upsetting in the extreme to be told that there was "nothing wrong" with him. The idea that his pains might be wholly imaginary tormented him. This time, however, one doctor was quite certain that he did, indeed, have lymphoma, or Hodgkin's disease. Another was quite certain that he did not, but both recommended that he cut down on his work and travel and not expose himself to severe climate.

At the annual mission meetings in Keswick, New Jersey, that year the huge problems of Evangelism-in-Depth were once again under consideration, and the directors were hard put to it to know whether to continue expanding or to retrench. One of the general council members revealed that he had been given the spirit of prophecy, and it was shown to him that Satan was attempting to obstruct the advance of the evangelistic effort by causing Ken Strachan's illness and convincing the other leaders that they were already carrying as heavy a burden as they could possibly bear. What God wanted was even

Instructing Colombian Christians in Corozal, 1963

Strachan talks with Victor Landero, Colombian lay evangelist

Strachan (*front*) with fellow missionary
and Colombian friends

Evangelism-in-Depth parade in Nicaragua, 1960

greater faith, larger efforts, new fields to conquer.

Ken was not present at the time of the prophecy, but was told of it, and wrote to the prophet, "I want to thank you for the word you brought from the Lord. . . . I want to go on and in a very egocentric way ask you some questions having to do with the bearing of your prophecy on my future and on my present state of health. The question of my importance to the cause of Evangelism-in-Depth is hardly worthwhile taking up. We have always had to proceed on the thesis that no man is indispensable and have always found that the Lord provided the necessary replacement.

"But I would like to know your thinking and have your counsel. The Lord can work through a sick man as well as a healthy one. But this business that I have—whatever it is—assails me at the oddest times with no rhyme or reason and leaves me so very weak I don't care what happens. Theologically I had long come to the conviction that divine healing is one of the gifts and/or signs that we could naturally expect from the Lord. I had always believed that in a time of need I would naturally have recourse to the Lord for such healing. I can't understand the complete sense of apathy which I have experienced on the subject ever since I myself came in need of it. Numberless friends like yourself have spoken to me. I have on occasion, more when I was in despair over the gnawing and debilitating symptoms of this sickness, called on the Lord for healing, but not in faith and not persistently.

"This may be an attack of Satan as you say (somehow, I have not been able to separate my present state of health from some strange incidents that took place in the southern wilds of our Colombia field just three weeks before the swollen nodes and lymph glands were discovered*—but other questions persist—Why. You yourself know the kind of whys that come to mind. I can't eliminate the possibility that this sickness is not an attack of Satan but one of chastisement (I Corinthians 11:30, 'It is this careless participation [in the Lord's supper] which is the reason for the many feeble and sickly Christians

---

* The incident referred to was the discovery one night while in his hammock of an "unusual sore" which he could not explain and took to be possibly an attack of Satan which God had permitted in the midst of a season of special spiritual uplift.

in your Church . . .' J. B. Phillips' translation). But here again, as to cause and solution, ignorance and apathy. . . .

"I would be interested in your thoughts about expanding Evangelism-in-Depth. And I covet your prayers for me, too. Apart from 1) a radical healing and 2) a fresh filling of the Holy Spirit accompanied by whatever gifts He chooses to impart, I see no future part for RKS in Evangelism-in-Depth."

Twenty-four years earlier, Ken had written to his fiancée, "What if some day I were as sick and as horrible-looking as he [a boy he had visited in the hospital]—would you want to care for me? I hope, dear, that I'll never be really sick. . . . We're so young and full of life that it's hard to think of ever being old and weak."

He was not yet prepared at fifty-four to think of himself as old and weak. Although quite certain by now that he had lymphoma, in torture with a cough, fever, swollen glands, and a persistent and nearly intolerable itching over his entire body, he wrote to Harry, "The best I can do is to tell you not to follow my example. . . . Remind yourself as I try to remind myself when I am in the troughs, that then is the time to discipline oneself to live and work by principle rather than emotion, by faith rather than feeling, by mind rather than stomach."

Elizabeth's circular letter to friends early in December said that Ken was still teaching his classes at Fuller, but tired rather quickly. His chief request was that the Lord would somehow use him in the midst of his weakness to help fellow workers, especially Latin American colleagues, in planning for the evangelistic efforts in Venezuela, Bolivia, and the Dominican Republic. Her letter closes with a poem from Hartley Coleridge (1796—1849),

> Pray if thou canst, with hope; but ever pray,
> Though hope be weak, or sick with long delay.

CHAPTER 16

The children were all coming out to Pasadena for Christmas. Ken thought about the things they would do together. Marie, in the seventh grade, and John, a junior in high school, were living with their parents, but the others were nearly grown up, and this would be a special Christmas for them. They could discuss things. The college kids would have questions and gripes and ideas, and they could all discuss them. They could play golf. Ken had several sets of clubs, and planned to buy another so that four of them could play at once. He told Elizabeth that this time he and she would do all the dishes. The children were always very good about helping at home, but this time they would not need to. Not that Ken liked doing dishes, but it was something he could do for his children. And there would be no lectures. He made it clear to Elizabeth that there would be no lectures of any kind. They would have family Bible study in the mornings—not too long, not preachy, but a give-and-take sort of thing, with hymn-singing. He wanted to get some Inter-Varsity hymnals so that each could have one. And they would go to whatever there was to go to in Los Angeles—concerts, plays, games, maybe even a movie if there was a good one. He saved money for this, and asked Elizabeth to inquire around as to what would be going on in town.

Then came the fever. Suddenly Ken's temperature shot up to 103. His face and neck began to swell, the aches in back and legs grew much worse, his body began to itch. His blood count, which had been very low for some time, went lower. Uremic poisoning was suspected this time, although the doctors knew, and had told the

Strachans, that there was no promise of a cure for lymphoma, and if he had been in remission he could expect a setback sometime. Somehow Ken had been sure that he would be all right for Christmas. They had prayed, with hope and without it. Friends had prayed, and things looked encouraging until the first week in December. He lay most of the day on a sofa in the living room, trying to read, even trying now and then to write something. He got up several times a day to walk back and forth in the room with John because he wanted to exercise.

"John," he said one day, "I'm not dead and I'm not alive. I'm sitting on the fence. We'll just have to wait and see how this comes out."

Shortly before Christmas the doctor ordered him into the hospital. For a man who, according to his wife, was "always a winner, always got what he wanted," this was a poor arrangement. It was not at all the Christmas he had planned. But the children came, and one by one arrived in his hospital room to find him looking small and weak and old, his gray hair white now and thin, his lips sore, his face puffy and red. From his usual weight of 165 pounds, he had sunk to 130. He was not fully in command of his emotions, and the sight of his children, looking on the body that was now such an embarrassment to him, was more than he could bear, and he cried.

Some of the plans he had cherished could be carried through. They had discussions, they read the Bible together, they sang hymns. The doctor was surprised to find them gathered on Christmas Day around Ken's bed, singing some of the simplest of Gospel songs— "Blessed assurance, Jesus is mine," "God will take care of you," "Just as I am, without one plea." But Ken's extreme weakness make it impossible to sustain any conversation for long, or to have too many in the room at once. After one exhausting day he learned that his son Robert had wished there were some way to talk to his father alone. "Get everybody out of here," Ken told Elizabeth. And Ken and Robert talked.

Clare spent a day and a night in his room, as did others, taking her turn to try to keep him from scratching. The itching had become so severe that even after heavy sedation, and wearing gloves, Ken would wake in the morning with his flesh raw. When Clare said,

"Daddy, stop it," he would open his eyes partway as if to say, "Where did you come from?" It was hard for Clare to have to tell her father what to do, and as she sat she thought of the nights when, as a little girl, she would waken and cry with the thought, "What if Daddy should die?" But during her visit to Pasadena she read the story of Lazarus, and she felt certain that God was not going to allow her father to die.

Cathy was studying to be a nurse, and Ken wanted her to attend him. Whatever she did was right. It was only to her, of all of his children, that he let himself ask the overwhelming question that was in his mind. "Do you think I'm going to make it?" She was not sure.

The children went back to school. Elizabeth virtually lived at the hospital. Sometimes John and Marie went in. More and more people began to pray for the recovery of Kenneth Strachan. One lady, a missionary under the LAM in San José, believed that God had given her a special task of praying for Ken. She was not merely to ask that he be healed. She was to believe absolutely, and never to waver in that belief, that he would be fully and completely cured. Scripture verses were "given" to her as proof of God's intention, and she held on so confidently that she did not even need to add "if it is Thy will" to her petitions. She knew that it was His will.

There were some nights when Elizabeth found her husband gripping the bedposts, sobbing, "I can't stand it." Once she left him and went out into the hall, unable to watch, and silently cried, "Lord, the meanest man in Pasadena would put a stop to this if he could!"

People came to the hospital to pray by his bedside, and there were times when it seemed inescapably clear that his suffering was in direct proportion to the amount of praying done over him.

Then, miraculously, he improved. Elizabeth had been sure she would never have him at home again, and suddenly the doctor said he could go home. Perhaps the prayers, which had seemed so futile, were actually effective. How could they have doubted God's love and power? Perhaps Ken's cancer was to be the exceptional case which would baffle the doctors and reward the faith of the hundreds who had besought God for his healing. God might, after all, have work for Ken to do.

Elizabeth fixed up a sunny corner of the living room. She put up fresh curtains for his homecoming and bought a new reclining chair. Ken was able again to write, and he sent a "medical bulletin" to his four children who were in school.

"Strachan came home on Thursday and was overwhelmed by the loving preparation that had been made by an extra-special someone for his return. Weighed in at 115 pounds, lost a pound next day. . . . For the present Dr. McLain does not allow me to go outdoors, so I divide my time between the bedroom and this lovely corner of the living room. On my left is the piano bench crowded with the books on Revelation II and III which I'm presently studying, and at my right Robin's stenophonic and the medley of sound provided by the records which you all assembled at Christmas. Harry, I'm thoroughly enjoying the Twentieth Century Folk Mass, and strangely enough, the Peter, Paul and Mary recording. Also, I thoroughly enjoy the Mormon Tabernacle Choir, Bev Shea's hymns, etc., not to mention the few classical selections that we have. And Mother has drawn out from the Public Library some of Bach and Brahms. So between the music and my studying, the days go by.

"You'll all be interested to know that this afternoon we had a telephone call from Billy Graham. He was phoning from the hospital where he had gone to see me. We gave him directions to our home and had a happy visit with him and T.W. and Grady Wilson. The first thing he did was to ask me what God had been saying to me through my experience of illness. When I had given a partial answer he said that he had stopped off on his way to Honolulu with only one purpose and that was to let me know that in every prayer for me (which he said was daily) that he had a strong assurance that God was going to heal me. He said that he did not pretend any absolute knowledge, that it was a mystic experience, and God might have something better for me, but he added that he had frequently experienced this sense of assurance in his praying.

"We talked quite a bit about God's dealing with his servants in suffering, and I think it was a revelation of Billy's character when he said that he envied me my experience, and knew that the Lord needed to teach him or bring him into closer fellowship through suffering. When I said that I never asked the Lord for healing but that I did ask for the filling of His Spirit with whatever gifts He would care to impart, Billy interrupted and said, 'Pray that for me also.'

"As you can imagine, these are days of lowest physical ebb, when the tide is just turning and a long, slow, hard pull looms ahead, so I have need of every encouragement. . . .

"I said to Mother the other day, 'I can never repay you,' and she answered, 'You can try!' So I guess we're back on the old footing.

"P.S. The last verses that struck me in the hospital were Psalm 118:17, 18: 'I shall not die, but live, and declare the works of the Lord. The Lord has chastened me sore, but he hath not given me over unto death,' and 27, 28: 'God is the Lord, which hath shewed us light; bind the sacrifice with cords, even unto the horns of the altar. Thou art my God and I will praise Thee: Thou art my God and I will exalt Thee.' "

A friend in Latin America received a letter from Ken asking him to pray for him. "All my hope is in the Lord," Ken wrote. The friend prayed, and thought that he heard God say to him, "When science fails, I will do a great thing."

Ken ate as much as he could to try to gain strength, and managed to put on four pounds. He paced the floor, he played Rook and Scrabble with Elizabeth, he listened to the records. At night, however, his temperature would go up, and the itching prevented his sleeping properly. But there was some improvement in muscle tone and skin color, and both Ken and Elizabeth were enormously encouraged. Ken began to plan a trip to Costa Rica in March. He wrote breezy notes to Dit, Dayton, and Dave, "If you guys want me to hang around some more and pester you you'd better bend your knees frequently." One of these memos was labeled, "Subject: Complaint." In it he said, "From some of the correspondence which I am joyfully receiving from many different members of the family in both Colombia and Costa Rica, I get the uneasy feeling that as a result of some of your reports (yes, you, HLF, WDR, and maybe DMH) that a heroic image of the way in which I am taking my sickness is unconsciously in the making.

"This is to remind you that I am, always have been, and undoubtedly will continue to be, a moaner and a groaner of the first water, and that I have no intention of giving up my prerogatives along this line. I think that we should be very careful lest unconsciously we create a symbol which no one, least of all I myself, can live up to. Right now I feel anything but heroic."

One visitor to his room said that to anyone who saw him suffer there could be no question that he was heroic. "The Lord has me on the griddle," Ken told more than one friend, "and I want Him to keep me there until He has taught me what He wants."

"I'm not demanding healing," he said to someone. "I'm only talking about what I want, as a child to his father."

Two friends who had just seen him were flying east together, talking about what they had seen. "Ken is dying," said one, "and apparently in darkness. He doesn't seem to have the least glimmer of light, or of the comfort so many saints have spoken of at death. I don't understand it."

A few days before the planned trip to Costa Rica Ken began to choke.

"If I go back to that hospital they'll never let me out," he protested, but his son Johnny took him for injections, and the doctors insisted he remain.

The days which followed were days of horror for Ken and for all who had to watch. The missionary in San José held on to her covenant with God—she would pray and Ken would be healed. Latin Americans, North Americans, Christians and people who would hardly have known enough to call themselves Christians, prayed in every way they knew. There were those who prefaced every prayer with 'If it be Thy will, Lord,' and there were those who were sure enough of His will to see no need for such a preface. Some came to his hospital room to pray, and some tense little battles were waged across his bed between those who felt that no Christian has an inalienable right to claim physical healing, and those who believed that such an admission was a mere failure of faith, or worse still, an actual capitulation to Satan himself who held the sufferer in his grasp. There were those who wished to anoint Ken with oil after the manner described in the Epistle of James, and those who asked to lay hands on him in prayer. He did not object to any of these gestures, although they sometimes made him feel surrounded by conflict and confusion. If his illness was in reality a diabolical attack he knew that he had better do some fervid praying and some strong resisting. If, on the other hand, it was a griddle on which God Himself had placed him in order to perfect in him the image of His Son, then his only obligation was to submit in trust and patience.

"Who am I, that I can yak and expect God to come and rescue me out of this situation?" was the way he felt when he talked to his sister. "We are not a privileged people, exempt from suffering." But he believed in the sovereignty of God, and knew that his own perspective was distorted. "Whatever my tiny contribution to God's pattern may be, He is a loving Father and looks upon me as His child."

A friend in whose home he had often stayed in Pasadena while on speaking trips was Margaret Jacobsen, who had been Elizabeth's roommate in college. She and her husband had provided a home for the Strachans next to their own, and they came often to the hospital while Ken was there. She wrote, "It would be untrue to say that the glory of the Lord pervaded that room and touched all that entered with ethereal blessing, but it would be equally untrue to fail to recognize the faithfulness of spirit with which Ken clung to Christ."

The itching, the swelling, the pain, and the choking went on. Ken went on "enduring the unendurable," and his friends went on praying.

On February 22, 1965, pulmonary involvement had become so extensive that Ken could hardly breathe. All his doctors were called in. To Elizabeth he looked like a "trapped animal." His frantic, pleading expression seemed to say to her, "Why aren't you *doing* something about this?" She stood, paralyzed with fear. "What should I be doing?" she thought. There was nothing that could be done that was not being done, and late that night friends persuaded Elizabeth to go home and sleep, while a friend of Ken's asked to be allowed to remain through the night at his bedside, praying.

The next morning Elizabeth woke with the knowledge that she would not leave the hospital again until Ken had died. A long day followed. In the morning Ken asked the friend who had prayed all night for him to read something from the Bible. He said little after that. The last words anyone remembers were, "I feel trapped."

Elizabeth sat beside him as he choked, gagged, struggled for breath, and finally sank into coma. It was too much for John, who asked to be allowed to leave. Late in the afternoon the doctor told Elizabeth that this would be it. Margaret Jacobsen offered to stay the night with her. Exhausted, Elizabeth fell asleep but at about two o'clock was awakened by choking sounds again, and in a few minutes Ken died.

The children were called, and Harry was on his way to Pasadena almost immediately. Friends came, flowers were sent, Harry made the funeral arrangements. The missionary who was praying in San José was told, "Ken is with the Lord," and found herself in confusion, with no answer to her questions. "Well, we don't have to have answers," she thought. Later that day she experienced a new love and trust for God, and He seemed to say to her, "All that you ask from now on you will receive. The firstfruits are Mine."

Harry prayed, "O God, help me to believe that underneath this all makes sense. . . . Help all of us whose lives were so closely tied to Daddy's to find in You what we need to fill the hole." He wrote in his journal, "The tears were running down the outside of my face, and unconsciously I almost said, 'God damn it!' and then, catching myself, thought, 'About death I can say "God damn it" and be agreeing with God.' Then in the early morning dark I felt strongly the 'enemy' in death. Then I thought of Jesus before Lazarus' tomb. I once heard that in the Hebrew it says He was *angry*."

Of a meal eaten together on the day after their father's death Harry wrote, "It was the same as so many other meals in the past. Paul [Roberts] was eating double portions and teasing Grandmother, who in her proper and dignified way was worrying over whether Marie had soup and why I wasn't eating. Marie and Johnny talked on normally laughing at Paul. Mother mentioned that the TV dinner was good, and so the conversation rambled on. Several things struck me: 1) the ever-going-on-ness of life. We come to the climax, the corner in the road. Time doesn't hesitate. The second or minute or hour of raw reality is no longer than any other and we keep on living, eating. 2) The way every person remained unchanged or himself at the table, and yet somehow the role, the traditional table ritual seemed a little askew, not quite what everyone wanted it to be."

There was a memorial service at Fuller Seminary with a packed-out attendance. Funds were given by many friends for Elizabeth and all the children to go to Costa Rica where Ken had asked to be buried, and the following day they flew with the body back to the little country where the other Strachans—Ken's mother and father and brother—were buried.

The casket was placed in a room at the seminary in San José, and the people began to come.

An old man whose daughters had grown up at the mission farm came with his cane and dark glasses, wearing slacks and a baggy sport coat, scarcely able to see well enough to get down the steps. He went up to Harry and shook hands, and then shuffled over to the casket and stood looking down at the body of his friend. Slowly he began to sob. Harry put a hand on his, and the old man said, "Don Kenneth was very good to me and my family," and turning away sat down and cried.

An old servant came and cried very loudly.

Latin men from several countries who had been deeply influenced by Strachan through the seminary, or through his traveling ministry, and who were now pastors and teachers, came.

One of the first girls Susan Strachan had enrolled in her new institute, now an elderly lady, came from San Salvador.

A buddy from childhood days in San José, with whom Ken had shared some lively escapades, came.

The missionaries, of course, came.

One after another spoke of Ken as his "closest friend."

Harry sat alone by the casket through the night, and in the morning a missionary came and spoke to him of the Resurrection. He knew the truth of her words. He saw, too, that his father's death could not be called a mystery.

"It was all very clear and straight and inevitable like the last act of a classic tragedy. Daddy's long-standing fight with life, the long trips, the heavy responsibility, the very building in which we were mourning in a sense was built with his sweat and agonized prayers. We had all known that his inability to take care of himself or to live easily would kill him long before the rest of us. The miracle was to expect that he could get through life without paying the bill."

The funeral service was held that afternoon in the Templo Bíblico, which Susan Strachan had built thirty-five years before. It was one of the largest funerals the city had ever seen—over three thousand attended.

"People were banked in every entrance and window, and even around the platform," Harry wrote. "The most moving part for me was the congregation's singing 'Cara a Cara' ('Face to Face with Christ'). They picked up the song and it rolled out strong and deep and harmonious. But they refused to keep up with the organ and it slowed to a deep, slow-moving expression of mourning that ended in the full-voiced tribute to their faith that 'face to face' we would all, like Daddy, see the Lord."

Harry had been asked to speak on behalf of the family. He spoke in Spanish, briefly and directly. He thanked the people for their comfort, love, and prayer. He spoke of how the sight of his father's casket at the airport, against the backdrop of Costa Rica's mountains, the tarpaulin which covered it blowing gently in the wind of the Meseta Central, reminded him that his father had come home— back to his own land, to his family, to his people. "We believe that this is a part of God's perfect plan for him, and is a part of His perfect plan for us and for the work which he carried in his heart.

"Just before He died, Christ said, 'It is finished.' Because the work of Christ was finished, Father was able to sing, 'Just as I am, without one plea but that Thy blood was shed for me.' But Father did not believe that his own work was finished. He died in the battle, with the impression that his enemy Death was closing doors of service which God Himself had opened for him. For this reason a passage in the book of Joshua has helped us who are his sons in the flesh and those who are his sons in the spirit: 'My servant Moses is dead. Get up now, and go over Jordan. As I was with Moses, so I will be with thee. I will never leave thee nor forsake thee.'"

The casket was carried for a mile and a half on the shoulders of a constantly rotated group of men. The crowd that followed filled the street solidly from wall to wall and stretched for several blocks behind. There was more singing at the cemetery, Juan Isais spoke, and the body was slid into the tomb and walled up.

It is the walling up that is the end of everything. Or so it seems. The tomb, like the life, is closed, sealed, silent. The "earthly dwelling is taken down, like a tent." But there were those in the crowd that day who watched the sealing of the stone and thought of the surprise that came to some others, a long time before, when they discovered that the seal was not permanent after all. If there was any basis at all for the faith that R. Kenneth Strachan had held through all of his life, this was not the end of everything. He had believed what Paul believed: "Truly, if our hope in Christ were limited to this life only we should, of all mankind, be the most to be pitied. But the glorious fact is that Christ did rise from the dead. . . . As members of the Christ of God all men shall be raised to life." Most of those who had loved Ken were able to hold onto this hope. "But if we hope for something we cannot see," Paul said, "then we must settle down to wait for it in patience."

It is the waiting that is hard. We cannot picture what is to come. We can only go back over what has gone, in the little space between womb and tomb, and try to understand what it means. We can think of what a man did—of what Ken Strachan did and failed to do, of what he hoped to do and will be done by others because of him. It is relatively easy to assess his life in terms of the judgments of his friends and associates ("a great missionary statesman," "a kind and humble man," "the foremost missionary thinker," "a man without pretension"), the testimonies of those he influenced ("he was a true saint"), the legacies he has left us (Evangelism-in-Depth has moved into forty countries now). Do such things bring us any closer to the real meaning of his life? (For the meaning of a particular life always raises the more profound question of the meaning of life itself.) And what of the inside story of this life—his heredity and environment, his personality with its strengths and flaws, his hopes fulfilled and unfulfilled, his prayers answered and unanswered, his decisions and escapes and rationalizations and successes, his doubts about himself, his confidence, his despair, his faith, his longings, his love? Is it here that we find the real meaning? He knew himself to be an "earthen vessel," but would hardly have claimed the other things Paul claims in that Bible passage—"handicapped on all sides, but never frustrated; puzzled, but never in despair; knocked down, but never knocked out." Ken knew himself to be frustrated as well as handicapped, despairing as well as puzzled, and at least once knocked out altogether. "Always exposed to death for Jesus' sake"—he knew that, too—"so that the life of Jesus may be plainly seen in our mortal lives"—he prayed for this, but was not sure of the answer. Others believed that they saw it in him. Who can say with any assurance? Can we even for an instant contemplate a life as God sees it, without sentimentality? Or will we, the instant we see clearly, lacerate ourselves either for looking through rose-colored glasses, or for judging without charity? Sentimentality is not compassion, for it is blind and ignorant. Compassion both sees and acknowledges the truth and accepts it, and perhaps God alone is wholly compassionate.

And God alone can answer the question, Who was he? In terms of God's story—the whole current of His thought regarding the world and the race of men He made—who was R. Kenneth Strachan?

The answer is beyond us. Here are the data we can deal with. There is much more that we do not know—some of it has been forgotten, some of it hidden, some of it lost—but we look at what we know. We grant that it is not a neat and satisfying picture—there are ironies, contradictions, inconsistencies, imponderables. The circumstances of his death alone, so far from crowning with glory a life of earnest endeavor to be a faithful servant, seemed the last mockery. (But perhaps significant in that very aspect—for did they not say to the Lord Himself, "He trusted in God—let Him deliver Him now!") There was no miraculous deliverance. The course of human events was run, the last farthing paid, without divine intervention.

Some who stood by and prayed and watched offered "explanations." These were mere anodynes. There were others who were struck dumb. Elizabeth was one of these, and she found a reason for hope in the words of George MacDonald:

I have no knowledge, wisdom, insight, thought
Or understanding fit to justify Thee in Thy work, O Perfect,
Thou hast brought me up to this and lo, what Thou hast wrought,
I cannot call it good. But I can cry,
O Enemy, *The Maker hath not done!*
One day thou shalt behold, and from the sight wilt run.

Here, then, is as much of the truth as one biographer could discover about a man. Let the reader find as much of its meaning as he can. Is it legitimate to ask whether the work for which this man is especially remembered is significant *at all* as the "true" work of God in and through him? Can we wonder whether there is any sense in which he especially "served" God? Was his work any more, or perhaps any less, noticeable to the angels than that of any man who loves God? Are all such categories spurious in the Real World? Will Kenneth Strachan have been welcomed home with a "Well done, good and faithful servant," or will he simply have been welcomed home? The son who delights the father is not first commended for what he has done. He is loved, and Kenneth Strachan was sure of this one thing. His favorite hymn was:

> Just as I am, without one plea
> But that Thy blood was shed for me,
> And that Thou bidst me come to Thee.
> O Lamb of God, I come.

> Just as I am, Thou wilt receive,
> Wilt welcome, pardon, cleanse, relieve,
> Because Thy promise I believe.
> O Lamb of God, I come.

This was his faith—not that he would have earned a place, or built temples or won great victories, but that God had accepted him because He had once become a man, and had lived through the tortures of being a man, and died the death of a man, in order to bring the lonely race of men, from all their deaths of whatever kind, Home.

1. OBEDIENCE

The Battle of the Pants

He was only seven years old, but even a man of that age has his dignity and self-respect to protect. To wear short pants when, in the new neighborhood to which he had moved, all the other boys his age were wearing long, was simply intolerable and unreasonable.

It was true that he had only one pair of long pants—his Sunday best. True also that another pair of everyday long ones would cost money. And he was ready to admit that on the mission field where he'd lived before, most of the boys had worn short pants. But that didn't change the fact that here nobody did. He just could not wear those short pants here.

For days, each morning, the boy and his mother fought the battle of the pants. In the end, overcome by the superior forces of an unyielding parent and faced with the grim alternatives of short pants or no pants, he had rebelliously pushed his legs through the hated shorts. But not without a last and telling shot.

"All right," he had sobbed, "I'll wear them. But when I get to heaven I'm going to ask God if a seven-year-old boy should wear long pants or short, and if He says long ones, you'll be sorry!"

The deep questions and hurts posed by the battle of the pants and the need for a ruling from heaven on what is indeed fitting for a seven-year-old in that situation are things of the past. At least for that particular boy. But for him and even his parents the same battle has to be fought and re-fought endlessly on different fronts and battle lines. And always, of course, the issues are not quite as simple as they appear to be on the surface. For what is involved is generally more than a free choice between long or short, or an innocent question of taste. Parental authority, social custom and relationships, personal liberty, ethics and morals and many other questions are also involved.

Also, unfortunately, in numberless matters not basic to our faith in Christ it is not always possible down here to secure that sure, final, authoritative word from on high that will resolve the doubts and settle the dust and strife of battle. True, we have God's Written Word—our final, infallible norm of truth and conduct. What a source of comfort and certitude it is; how simple and clear on the way of salvation; how wonderful a lamp to our feet! How wonderful it would be if we could all understand it perfectly and agree as to all its teaching, not only regarding the essentials, but also in its concepts of lesser significance.

But for the present, confronted with the many shades of opinion, taste custom, tradition, culture, judgment and interpretation, and faced with the contradictory claims of Biblical sanction for each, it is rather vexing indeed that these matters cannot be settled once and for all. Or that, having settled them ourselves, others are so slow and reluctant to accept the light. How frustrating to have to wait till we get to heaven for the verdict which will enable us to say, "I told you so."

In the meantime, perhaps, we'll have to accept the counsel of the Apostle to "let every man be fully persuaded in his own mind," and so seek ourselves to walk with clean consciences toward both God and men. This can be applied to missions, to churches and their relationships, as well as in matters of personal conscience and ethic.

It might be a help to all of us, the old as well as young, the strong and wise as well as the weak and foolish, to learn to distinguish the things that differ, to avoid confusing the customs and traditions of man with the Word of God, to avoid mistaking aesthetics for ethics, culture for godliness, and the possibly necessary but temporary and local for the essential eternal and universal.

And we need to remember with humility that for the present our knowledge is imperfect—we see in a mirror dimly, we know only in part—and that therefore the law of boundless love must govern us in all these things.

In the end, so many of our differences and wrangles which we now claim to be so crucial and important may turn out to have been of as little enduring consequence as the long-forgotten "battle of the pants."

Editorial by R. Kenneth Strachan in *Latin America Evangelist*, May-June 1961. Reprinted by Permission.

2. LONELINESS

Apartado 936
Guatemala, C. A.
July 29, 1962

My dear Clare:

Because you are very much on my mind and because I love you in a special way tonight, I want to drop you a special private line before I try to write a general letter to the four of you. I want you to know how much I admire your grit and purposefulness in working this summer.

Right now with Aunt Minnie away on vacation you may be finding it a little lonesome. I'll never forget the lonesomeness I experienced when my dad and mother left me alone in Kansas City, Mo. for one whole year while they surveyed South America. I was only ten, and the Weavers who took care of me couldn't have been nicer to me. But some Sunday nights when they went off to church I would stay alone in the house and as the darkness and silence settled over the house, it was hard not to feel completely desolated. Maybe because of that experience I've always dreaded lonesomeness almost more than anything else. I know that it causes one of the deepest and sharpest agonies that humans are called to experience.

But the fact of the matter is that all of us are called to face loneliness at many points in the course of our lives—and specially if we follow the "Man of Sorrows". So I have been thinking that perhaps the Lord may allow these two weeks to be a time of loneliness for you in order to teach or begin to teach a lesson which could be the most valuable in all your life. And that is to learn that real loneliness is not a matter of space or solitude. For if we can learn to be alone by ourselves and enjoy a sense of fellowship with the Lord, then we'll never be lonely in all our lives, no matter what comes. For you can never be sure of having forever the kind of company that husband or wife or family provides.

I don't know whether you will find the following quotation too deep or not, but I have found it helpful for me and would like to pass it on to you:

"Loneliness arises not from isolation in spirit . . . Loneliness results in part from the illusion sinful man indulges that he can live with other persons without committing himself to share in their concerns, or entering into a responsible interdependence. . . .

The walls between persons which are created by our culture can only be scaled by the kind of concerned love that does care and share. The deepest needs in human life are met by love and acceptance."

All of which has served me as a reminder that unless I give myself to others (and not necessarily alone to the kind of people I instinctively like or would want to choose for my friends) that then, regardless of my physical surroundings and no matter how many people are in the house I live in, I'm doomed to experience the frightfulness and frustration of loneliness. But as long as there are human beings to whom I can relate in some sort of outgoing and self-giving, and as long as there is a Loved and Loving One who seeks to meet me in the fellowship of the "hidden room", I need never know loneliness though in His will I may often know solitude.

Clare dear, much much love,

Daddy

3. WOMANLINESS

San Jose de la Montaña
Sunday-Dec. 22, 1963

Dear . . . . . .:

A week ago yesterday I was performing the wedding ceremony in the Templo for . . . . and . . . . Last night . . . . and . . . . were married in the Seminary chapel and it was my responsibility to give the bride away. After the reception in the dining room, Mother and I drove . . . . . . and . . . . . . up to the farm where they are spending the week-end.

As I escorted . . . . . . up the aisle in all her wedding finery, I thought to myself—one of these days I may be doing the same thing for . . . . . . I wonder if I'll be nervous. And before we head up the aisle, I wonder if I'll have the opportunity to talk with her about marriage. I thought—probably not, she'll be in such a frenzy getting ready and in any case its always so difficult to try to express the thoughts you have. That's when I began to think that I would write you a letter and entitle it "Ah Sweet Mystery of Life" or something like that from a well-meaning bumbling father to a daughter whom he loves and admires.

But it's not going to be so much about how to make a success of marriage—that lecture you'll probably get out of the many books on the subject and in any case you'll have to learn the ropes as you go along. It's just going to be about one aspect of marriage—how to find the man or rather how to manage to be found by the right man.

I suppose there's an awful lot involved in getting ready for a wedding. When do you begin to start? By the time . . . . . . wedding march began to sound and after some twenty *parejas de padrinos,* half a dozen maids of honor, and several flower girls (including . . . . . .) had gone down the aisle, she was one bundle of nerves and weariness. She faced so many problems and had so many details to attend to. But actually the ceremony was over in less than an hour and I realized then that all the fuss for the ceremony was relatively unimportant. What really *was* important —was something that had taken place before—that made *her,* rather than her twin sister . . . . . ., sought out and proposed to. And I don't suppose that either she or . . . . . . or . . . . . . could define or describe what it was.

What is it that draws a man to a particular woman? I'm not sure that anyone can pin it down. That's part of the "sweet mystery" of life. Anyone can list all the qualities that he wants in a wife. But that mysterious thing that does the trick is never merely the sum of all those qualities. It's an elusive thing that probably includes many things—something about her face that makes it easy to get accustomed to, the way she walks, the look in her eyes, her smile, her figure—and so much more. You can't define it, but you can't miss it. And of course it varies for each different man.

And the amazing thing is you can look around and see scores of lovely girls so superior in looks and personality to scores of wives, and yet they're still single. Perhaps it's from choice, but you wonder why. And you know that many of them are missing out on that "sweet mystery of life". Why?

I'm not sure that I can answer, but this is really why I wanted to write you, dear. Because it seems to me such an important factor in helping a girl be found by the right man and in holding him too. Right now, perhaps, you may not really be interested in getting serious about marriage with anyone—but sooner or later you will. And if you haven't somehow discovered the secret, then you may miss out later on.

One help, I think, is to realize what a man is looking for. No man can really define it, but I think that at heart we're all somewhat romantic, and that in the struggle which each one of us has with himself and with the world against which he must make good, he is always on the lookout for that woman who somehow embodies and will represent for him the mysterious provision that is "woman"—sweetheart, wife, mother, partner, companion, harbor in the storm—the helpmate that will fill up the inner emptiness and loneliness of a man's life, the one who'll stand at his side and encourage him in his fight and yet at the same time appeal to his sense of protectiveness and make him feel that he is a *man*. And it takes a *woman*—not a clothes horse, or a musician, or a doll, or a brilliant conversationalist but a *woman*, a daughter of Eve.

Now how on earth can a girl convey this idea of womanhood to a man? That's something she'll have to work on for herself. I'm not sure I can tell, but I'm sure that to the extent that a girl becomes representative of or embodies *womanhood* to that extent she becomes attractive to a man in the sense that leads him to the altar. The girl who uses sex as bait will attract a man but only for sexual satisfaction not for lifetime marital happiness. The girl who merely offers "palship" will probably have many male friends for a while until they drop off one by one to marry someone else.

Not every girl is endowed to bowl over every man she meets. But every girl has this one tremendous thing working for her—she is a *woman.* And the important thing is for her to be conscious of that and live up to it. How to do that is an art each girl has to develop. But she'd better work at it while she has time and circumstances in her favor. Speaking as a man, I think a girl is more attractive when she's a little on the quiet and reserved side. Most men shy away from the excessive talker.

I don't know anything that destroys more quickly the sense of "mystery" in womanhood, than excessive talk. And that doesn't mean that a man wants an enigmatic Mona Lisa—a somebody out of this world for a wife. But on the other hand you can't overlook or discount the tremendous appeal of a Mona Lisa—precisely because somehow (she may be an old cow and dumb as a horse) she embodies the mystery of womanhood.

Another thing is for a girl not to flock always to other girls—that's one sure way of "protecting" herself from the other sex.

Bueno, this has gone on long enough and probably isn't needed. So I would gather from your last letter. On the other hand, ... dear, I somehow can't forget the night you, ... and I drove back from Elgin. You talked the entire distance about the horseplay and fun you girls had in the dorm playing tricks on each other—of some interest to your fond papá, but absolutely a superb way to snuff out any romantic interest on the part of a boy—I think.

. . . . . . —I love your Irish ways—and one of these days I'll be the proud but nervous father strutting down that aisle. Keep up the good work at W R U.

Love, Dad

4. SEX

From a letter (undated) addressed to the oldest three Strachan children.

I've been thinking of writing you about different things from time to time—things that I wished someone had spoken to me about when I was your age. However I don't want you to feel that you're being preached at or that you have to read what I say. So if you feel like skipping this part of the letter, go ahead. I want to talk about one of the motive powers or forces that affect human beings—you and I too—and impels them to do and to be what they do and are. (Have you ever thought about some of these forces? Hunger, for instance? It makes you head for the dining room about three times a day or oftener. You take it for granted, but just try going without food for a while and you'll see how strong a force it is. Starving men will do almost anything for food, even to killing and eating each other—that's how strong a force it is. So hunger, just plain physical hunger is one of the principal forces that moves the world today, affecting us not only physically but also socially and politically—in every way.)

The force I want to talk to you about is almost as strong and in a sense is very much like Hunger. It's popularly called Sex—but it consists of more than just the physical instinct that is generally called Sex. It includes a deep desire to love and be loved that can only be satisfied in a very intimate relationship with one person of the other sex—the mating instinct that you see not only in human beings but in animals as well. But it goes deeper than that and I'm not sure that anyone can really describe all that it involves. It touches the very well-springs of creativity in each one of us, the deep longing for companionship, for reproducing ourselves, the need that each one of us feels for comfort and protection, and so on. I think that you each know what I mean even though it is something that you have only begun to be aware of in the last few years of your lives.

Now most books or lectures on the subject try to prepare you for courtship and marriage and perhaps none of you are quite ready for that, although you should, of course, be forewarned so as to avoid the many pitfalls and accidents that can spoil one's life before one finally finds the right mate and marches down the aisle to the tune of "Here comes the bride, big fat and wide". Both Mother and I want to fulfill our responsibility to you all by helping you know all that you should know about these matters at the right time, and we want you to feel perfectly free to ask us any questions that you may have. By all means, don't ever feel that these things are so secret and intimate that one never talks about them. They are intimate and very precious and people of good taste and breeding just don't go around making them coarse by crude talk, but that doesn't mean that you shouldn't know about them or come to those you trust for such information. So you feel free to write and ask, when the time comes that you feel that you should know.

But I don't intend to go into that part of it in this letter. What I want to write about is the part that that force which we call Sex plays in our lives apart from the normal activities of courtship and mating—the part it plays in our subconscious thoughts and desires, in the temptations that begin to come upon us and that drive and torment us not only when we're young and just starting out but even as we grow older and when we would have expected to have been freed from such temptations.

To me it has been helpful to recognize that Sex is one of the necessary powers or forces that God has instilled in us. You have it clearly indicated in the very beginning when God created man. Look up Genesis 1:27-28 and 2:18-25. And compare Eph. 5:25-33 and note that the mysterious force that brings man and woman together is so holy and beautiful that it is compared to the power that unites us to Christ. Now if Sex is such a tremendous force or power within us, then we must seek to understand how it works. For like Hunger or Electricity, it can work for us, for our enjoyment and satisfaction or for our hurt and unhappiness. So here are a few truths about this force that may be of some help to you in your own lives: (Have you noticed that each one of us has to live his life himself and that no one else can really do it for us?)

First, Sex just like any other God-given desire *is good.* That means that you don't have to be afraid of it or ashamed of it. "What God has cleansed, call not thou unclean." Just like Hunger is a normal thing indicative of physical health and well-being (It's a sick man who isn't hungry.) so with Sex. And just as the God-given appetite for food was meant to be satisfied, so with the God-given instinct for Sex.

Second, though good and God-given, Sex is not the only force or power that moves and makes human life. There are many others. Physical hunger of which I've already spoken is also only one of them. But as wonderful as it is to sit down to a nice juicy tenderloin steak nicely done, just think how poor and barren life would be if it were only a matter of eating? How you would come to hate beefsteaks and all the activity of eating if that's all you could do. But along with the sheer delight of football or any other sport, reading, art, music, human companionship, working toward specific goals, and above all fellowship with the Lord Himself, a nice juicy steak is a good thing. So with Sex. It's one of the great moving forces that affect us but only one among others. And one of the greatest mistakes we can make—and some kids make it—is to forget that it is only one and to let it become dominant in their lives, thus depriving them of the full enjoyment not only of the other forces but of Sex itself.

Third, Sex, like Hunger or any other instinct, can be perverted or diverted from its proper use or function. And that unfortunately is what has been done by the great mass of people in the world today. All the glorification of Sex in the movies, magazines, radio and television, theater, etc. contributes to that. You see it's such a strong instinct within each of us that we act like hungry people. Regardless of whether it is right or wrong, we seek for ways to satisfy that instinct. And when it gets out of place then it becomes lust and what was essentially right and good becomes sinful and wrong. That appetite can seek to be satisfied in all sorts of wrong ways, looking at sensual pictures in magazines or reading sex-filled literature, or trying to fool around with those of the other sex, or as Romans points out (1:26-27), perverting completely the use of sex. And the important thing to remember is that any perversion of Sex, whatever it may be, can never lead to proper joy and satisfaction because of the very fact that it is a perversion.

Fourth, To Sex as to everything else there is a time. (Eccles. 3:1-8) "To every thing there is a season and a time to every purpose under the heaven". And as our Lord showed us in the temptation in the wilderness, there can be in God's purpose for us, a time of fasting as well as a time of feeding on the bread. And so with Sex. The important thing is to make sure of God's time.

And that brings me to the *Fifth* point, which is that Sex just as much as any other phase of our lives must be turned over to the Lord. Your Mother has written an excellent article in *His* magazine for the month of March on prayer and wedding bells. Read it and you will realize that in our sex life as in everything else, "Thou wilt shew me the path of life; in Thy presence is fulness of joy: at Thy right hand there are pleasures forevermore."

This has already become far longer and windier than I intended. But as I said before you don't have to read it. But just know that both Mother and I are praying for this aspect of your lives as well as all the others, and our great desire is that in this as well as the rest you may each grow up to give God the best and to find in Him the best.

Much Love, kiddos,
Dad

Format by Katharine Sitterly
Set in Linotype Electra
Composed, printed and bound by The Haddon Craftsmen, Inc.
HARPER & ROW, PUBLISHERS, INCORPORATED